# Gethsemane

# Gethsemane

ANDREW C. SKINNER

DESERET
BOOK

SALT LAKE CITY, UTAH

**Library of Congress Cataloging-in-Publication Data**

Skinner, Andrew C., 1951–
  Gethsemane / Andrew C. Skinner.
    p.    cm.
  Includes bibliographical references and index.
  ISBN 978-1-57008-866-7 (alk. paper)
  1. Atonement.   2. Church of Jesus Christ of Latter-day Saints—Doctrines.
I. Title.
  BX8643.A85 S55   2002
  232'.3—dc21                                 2002013921

Printed in the United States of America
Publishers Printing, Salt Lake City, Utah

10  9   8   7   6   5   4   3   2

*For my family and friends,*
*who have taught me much*
*about the Atonement*

# Contents

# Introduction

Years ago I found myself sitting behind a desk in our ward meetinghouse, a young bishop trying to figure out what the Lord wanted done and how he wanted me to do it. Across the room from me was a thirteen-year-old young woman (I'll call her Brittany) who had many physical and developmental challenges. To this day she remains in my mind's eye tiny and frail. Her parents had insisted that she be baptized, even though, in my view, she did not need baptism because of her mental disabilities—the Atonement was already operating in her life.

Thankfully, I remembered some counsel given by a Church leader about compassion, and I listened to Brittany's parents' request that she be interviewed for baptism. I say thankfully because that evening Brittany taught me the lesson of a lifetime. It was an experience I shall never forget.

The interview did not start out well, nor did it improve as the minutes passed. I asked Brittany question after question that she could not answer the way I thought she should be able to. She could not talk about the first principles and ordinances of the gospel the way all the other Primary children had been able to, at least up to that point in my short tenure as bishop. She could not tell me why baptism is performed or how one is supposed to perform it. I grew frustrated and, I think, so did she. We were both miserable. I began to feel vindicated in thinking we didn't need to be in this interview. It was, after all, eating up valuable time I could have been using to "save" those who really needed it—couples with failing marriages, teenagers with moral challenges, and a host of other problems.

As I was about to abandon the interview, out of the corner of my eye I glimpsed a picture that the previous bishop had left hanging on the office wall. It was a framed print of the Savior in Gethsemane. At that instant the thought came into my mind, *Why don't you ask her who that picture represents?*

I had sense enough to follow the impression, even though my attitude wasn't in harmony with the nature of the question. I said to Brittany, "Do you know who this is?" as I pointed to the painting of the Savior, but my tone or inflection or demeanor or something made it sound like, "I'll bet you don't even know who this is!"

In a scene that remains frozen in my mind, I saw Brittany stand on her crippled feet, shuffle across the floor on the sides of her shoes, plop her hands down on the surface of my desk, lean towards me so that her face was directly in front of mine, only inches away, and say with deliberate and careful articulation, "That's Jesus—and he loves us!" To emphasize her point, Brittany lifted one of her hands off the desk, drew a circle in the air while at the same time nodding her head and saying, "All of us!"

I sat stunned. How was Brittany able to teach such a profound lesson? Fortunately, she drew the circle big enough to include me, for it was clear to me that at that moment I did not deserve to be in the circle with her. Her words convicted me as well as lifted and blessed me, all in the same instant.

"He loves us." The meaning and message of Jesus' experience in Gethsemane are that simple: he loves us—all of us. That is precisely the reason he went to Gethsemane as well as to Golgotha: love—love for his Father, love for his Father's children, love for leaders in his Church, love for all his humble followers, love for the entire human family, and, indeed, love for each one of us as individuals. He went to Gethsemane not only to redeem Brittany from the birth defects that left her unable to explain the fine points of baptism but also to ransom me from my narrow-minded, self-important impatience and deficient behavior. He went to Gethsemane for Brittany and me and literally billions and billions of others of our Father's children.

Jesus' experience with the bitter cup that terrible night in Gethsemane changed me the night of my interview with Brittany. That night in the bishop's office, Gethsemane became very personal. Because the Savior drank the bitter cup, because he squarely faced the bitterest of experiences in Gethsemane nearly two thousand years ago, all my own bitter experiences can become sweet. That is what happened the evening of my interview with Brittany. I am persuaded that others, unseen but very real, were looking in on us.

It is fair to say that Gethsemane became a focal point of my thinking and study, one that invited me to explore its significance as explained in the scriptures. I have come to appreciate that both Gethsemane and Golgotha were critical to the Father's plan, that Gethsemane had to come before Golgotha, and that Gethsemane is a much more significant part of the Savior's atoning sacrifice than some of us might have realized. The thoughts and ideas that follow have come from my explorations in the scriptures and in the writings of latter-day prophets and apostles.

*And now, behold, I will testify unto you of myself that these things are true. Behold, I say unto you, that I do know that Christ shall come among the children of men, to take upon him the transgressions of his people, and that he shall atone for the sins of the world; for the Lord God hath spoken it.*

*For it is expedient that an atonement should be made; for according to the great plan of the Eternal God there must be an atonement made, or else all mankind must unavoidably perish; yea, all are hardened; yea, all are fallen and are lost, and must perish except it be through the atonement which it is expedient should be made.*

ALMA 34:8–9

# CHAPTER 1

# Gethsemane and the Bitter Cup

Because each one of us is in very deed a daughter or son of divine parents, we ought to care very much about Gethsemane. All of our Heavenly Father's planning and preparation, all of his interest in his children and all of his desires for them, all of his aims and goals for the entire universe came down to a singular moment in a specific time and place on this earth in a garden called Gethsemane. Without Gethsemane in God's eternal plan, everything else would have been a colossal waste—*everything*. Without the events involving one particular Man in that olive vineyard almost two thousand years ago, God's purposes would have been utterly frustrated. Sin, death, decay, destruction, hell, and endless torment would reign supreme forever and ever. If Gethsemane had turned out to be a place associated with suffering and failure rather than suffering and triumph, everything that went before and everything that came afterward would have been reduced to a series of meaningless events in the eternal scheme of things, for there would be no eternal life. Deterioration, disorder, and chaos would ultimately fill the vastness of the universe; all beauty, human kindness, refinement, and acts of goodness would be forgotten as wasted energy. Truly, Gethsemane was the place where eternity hung in the balance.

## GETHSEMANE, THE ATONEMENT, AND RENEWAL

The events that occurred in Gethsemane were part of the atonement of Jesus Christ—not preparatory to it, nor secondary to it, but at the very heart of it. Without the Savior's unique and unparalleled redemptive activity in Gethsemane, there could have been no atonement, no reprieve from the relentless degenerative effects of sin, and, ultimately, no resurrection to eternal life beyond the Savior's own. Hence, physical and spiritual deterioration could never have been reversed. The pervasive, perpetual degeneration of our universe that is a result of the fall of Adam would not have been halted.

The redemption brought about by events in Gethsemane and the redemption brought about by the Resurrection fit together in complementary fashion. The Savior had "life in himself" (John 5:26) and thus power over his own death. But it was his substitutionary payment in Gethsemane for the fall of Adam and for our sins, together with his resurrection, that gave *us* lasting power over death. Gethsemane was as essential to salvation as Golgotha and the Garden Tomb. Gethsemane brought into existence the opportunity for all of Heavenly Father's children to experience spiritual rebirth, newness of life, and the renewal, rejuvenation, and cleansing of spirit bodies, just as resurrection brings about the renewal, even the re-creation, of physical bodies and establishes them as indestructible material entities. Both kinds of redemption are necessary. Golgotha and the Garden Tomb would mean nothing to us without Gethsemane.

Scientists tell us that the natural order of things in our universe is an irrevocable, steady movement toward decay: from life to death, from organization to chaos, from a condition or state of lesser degeneration to one of greater degeneration (a concept called entropy). This state of being is true for all kingdoms and creations—animals, plants, planets, stars, and other systems. Without Christ's atonement, human beings *and* the worlds on which they reside would be locked forever in the vise grip of death and dissolution. But with and through Christ's atonement, all things are made new. The process of decay is not only halted but reversed. Because of the Atonement, which includes events in Gethsemane as well as the universal resurrection, all things in the universe are empowered, renewed, and revitalized. Thus, Christ is the light and the *life* of the world.

If that godly Being named Jesus had not both lived a perfect life *and* had "life in himself," which attribute was genetically passed on to him by his Father in Heaven, he would not have had power over death, nor the physical capacity to endure the deathly horrors of Gethsemane, nor the ability to determine the time of his own decease while hanging on the cross, nor the capability to rise from the dead, nor the ability to pass on the power of regeneration to others. All men, women, and children would have remained subject to sin and its author forever. In truth, all would have become like the devil, even angels to the devil (2 Nephi 9:5–10). What the Savior *was* (the literal Son of God, having life in himself) gave him power over death for himself. What the Savior *did* (paying vicariously for the transferred sin and suffering of others in Gethsemane) gave him power over death for others.

## THE ATONEMENT AND ALL LIVING THINGS

So extensive and intensive is the atonement of Jesus Christ that this planet Earth is itself redeemed and sanctified by the same atoning power that redeems and sanctifies individual human beings. This concept has been revealed to God's prophets in all ages. Enoch testified that the earth is a living entity and requires the redemptive power of the Savior just as human beings do:

> And behold, Enoch saw the day of the coming of the Son of Man, even in the flesh; and his soul rejoiced, saying: The Righteous is lifted up, and the Lamb is slain from the foundation of the world; and through faith I am in the bosom of the Father, and behold, Zion is with me.

> And it came to pass that Enoch looked upon the earth; and he heard a voice from the bowels thereof, saying: Wo, wo is me, the mother of men; I am pained, I am weary, because of the wickedness of my children. When shall I rest, and be cleansed from the filthiness which is gone forth out of me? When will my Creator sanctify me, that I may rest, and righteousness for a season abide upon my face? (Moses 7:47–48)

The patriarch Abraham learned that the fall of Adam and Eve was so powerful that when our first parents fell, the earth also fell, or moved—from its position near Kolob, which is "nigh unto the throne of God" (Abraham 3:9) to its present location in our solar system (Abraham 5:13). But the atonement of Christ is infinitely more powerful than the Fall, and the earth will someday be physically moved back into the presence of God by the power of God (the Atonement). The Prophet Joseph Smith said, "This earth will be rolled back into the presence of God, and crowned with celestial glory" (*Teachings of the Prophet Joseph Smith,* 181).

President Brigham Young was even more detailed in his description of the physical fall and the redemption of this earth:

> When the earth was framed and brought into existence and man was placed upon it, it was near the throne of our Father in heaven. . . . But when man fell, the earth fell into space, and took up its abode in this planetary system, and the sun became our light. When the Lord said—"Let there be light," there was light, for the earth was brought near the sun that it might reflect upon it so as to give us light by day, and the moon to give us light by night. This is the glory the earth came from, and when it is glorified it will return again unto the presence of the Father, and it will dwell there, and these intelligent beings that I am looking at, if they live worthy of it, will dwell upon this earth. (*Journal of Discourses,* 17:143)

In a revelation so sublime it was designated "The Olive Leaf," Joseph Smith gave us another glimpse of just how much the atonement of Christ is tied to the physics of the universe and just how little we know about the greatest of the many powers operating in the cosmos. Because of the atonement of Christ, our earth will not only be physically changed, renewed, and receive a paradisiacal glory (Article of Faith 10) but will be crowned with celestial glory in the very presence of God the Father:

And the redemption of the soul is through him that quickeneth all things, in whose bosom it is decreed that the poor and the meek of the earth shall inherit it.

Therefore, it [the earth] must needs be sanctified from all unrighteousness, that it may be prepared for the celestial glory;

For after it hath filled the measure of its creation, it shall be crowned with glory, even with the presence of God the Father;

That bodies who are of the celestial kingdom may possess it forever and ever; for, for this intent was it made and created, and for this intent are they sanctified. (D&C 88:17–20)

In other words, because of the incomprehensible power of the Atonement not only is the earth redeemed and sanctified but it is destined to become the eternal abode and inheritance of all people who are similarly redeemed and sanctified by the very same atoning power of Jesus Christ. Thus, the Atonement connects people and planets in a seamless web of creation and redemption. In fact, every creature which fills the measure of its creation is likewise blessed by the power of the Atonement to inherit the kingdom of the Father's glory. Of the different beasts portrayed in the book in the Bible entitled The Revelation of St. John the Divine (Revelation 4:6–9; 5:13), the Prophet Joseph Smith said they were examples of the many varied creatures in heaven redeemed by God:

I suppose John saw beings there of a thousand forms, that had been saved from ten thousand times ten thousand earths like this,—strange beasts of which we have no conception: all might be seen in heaven. . . . John learned that God glorified Himself by saving all that His hands had made, whether beasts, fowls, fishes or men; and He will glorify Himself with them.

Says one, "I cannot believe in the salvation of beasts." Any man who would tell you that this could not be, would tell you that the revelations are not true. John heard the words of the beasts giving glory to God, and understood them. God who made the beasts could understand every language spoken by them. The four beasts were four of the most noble animals that had filled the measure of their creation, and had been saved from other worlds. (*Teachings of the Prophet Joseph Smith*, 291–92)

The atonement of Christ is so great in its effects and so far-reaching in its consequences that it easily qualifies as the most important occurrence in time or in all eternity. Nothing ever has or ever will surpass it in significance. Nothing is greater in the entire universe or in the history of created things than Christ's atonement. In Hebrew, the word *atonement* is rendered as *kippur* (as in *Yom Kippur*, "Day of Atonement"), which derives from the root *kaphar*, meaning "to cover." This is an apt connotation, for the atonement of Christ "covers" all things. "When the prophets speak of an *infinite* atonement, they mean just that. Its effects cover all men, the earth itself and all forms of life thereon, and reach out into the endless expanses of eternity" (McConkie, *Mormon Doctrine*, 64).

Thus, the atonement of Christ is infinite in time, space, and quantity—infinite in scope and eternal in duration. All death is answered; every creature under the Savior's dominion is resurrected. All sin is compensated for; every combination of sins is covered. The Atonement goes beyond personal sin to include

11

disappointment, sorrow, and suffering caused by the sins of others. It even extends to the sicknesses and infirmities we must bear just because we are mortal (Alma 7:11–12). It was made by a being who was God before he came to earth, who was the Son of God on earth, and who will be God eternally and endlessly.

## THE ATONEMENT AND THE UNIVERSE

Most stunning of all, the infinite atonement of Christ, worked out on this earth, extends to all worlds which Christ created under the direction and tutelage of God the Father—and that includes "worlds without number" (Moses 1:33). This sweeping aspect of the infinite atonement was revealed to the Prophet Joseph Smith and recorded in Doctrine and Covenants 76, a revelation so powerful and profound it is called simply the Vision. In this revelation the Prophet and Sidney Rigdon bear ultimate and irrefutable witness of the Savior's reality as well as his expansive *creative* power:

> And now, after the many testimonies which have been given of him, this is the testimony, last of all, which we give of him: That he lives!
>
> For we saw him, even on the right hand of God; and we heard the voice bearing record that he is the Only Begotten of the Father—
>
> That by him, and through him, and of him, the worlds are and were created, and the inhabitants thereof are begotten sons and daughters unto God. (D&C 76: 22–24)

Next they describe the extent of his *redeeming* power:

> That he came into the world, even Jesus, to be crucified for the world, and to bear the sins of the world,

and to sanctify the world, and to cleanse it from all unrighteousness;

That through him *all* might be saved whom the Father had put into his power and made by him. (D&C 76:41–42; emphasis added)

From the panoramic vision given to Moses, we begin to glimpse the magnitude and meaning of the statement that *all* are saved which the Father put into the Savior's power and made by him: "And *worlds without number* have I created; and I also created them for mine own purpose; and by the Son I created them, which is mine Only Begotten" (Moses 1:33; emphasis added). Remember how the Prophet Joseph Smith described it: "ten thousand times ten thousand earths like this [one]."

The doctrine of the all-encompassing nature of the Atonement was taught by Joseph Smith as part of his poetic rendering of Doctrine and Covenants 76. He reworked it into a poem which he composed in response to a poem penned by his friend W. W. Phelps. The portion of the Prophet's inspired rendition that corresponds to verses 22 through 24 reads as follows:

> And I heard a great voice, bearing record
>     from heav'n,
> He's the Saviour and only begotten of God—
> By him, of him, and through him, the worlds
>     were all made,
> Even all that career in the heavens so broad.
>
> Whose inhabitants, too, from the first to the
>     last,
> Are sav'd by the very same Saviour of ours;

And, of course, are begotten God's daughters
   and sons,
By the very same truths, and the very same
   pow'rs.
(*Times and Seasons* 4 [1 February 1843]: 82–83)

The Prophet Joseph Smith's singular witness of the Lord's living reality, his divine Sonship, and his creative workmanship also implies that the Creation is still going on. Joseph Smith learned what God revealed to Moses: "For behold, there are many worlds that have passed away by the word of my power. And there are many that now stand, and innumerable are they unto man; but all things are numbered unto me, for they are mine and I know them" (Moses 1:35). The Atonement covers all these worlds; Gethsemane was ordained that they might be redeemed. The power and wisdom exercised by Jesus are beyond the grasp of mortals. The written declarations of prophets about the creation and redemption of millions of earths by Christ through the same power that is held by the Father is testimony enough of Jesus' stature before his birth as the mortal Messiah. But such testimony is made visual when one stands outdoors on a clear, cloudless night to gaze into the star-filled heavens and realize that the vast expanse of the visible universe is only a small part of the Savior's realm.

Astronomers tell us that our solar system is located in a spiral arm of the Milky Way Galaxy, a flat, disc-shaped cluster of stars approximately 100,000 light years across at its widest point. A light year is the distance light travels in one year. Moving at the speed of 186,000 miles per second, a beam of light traverses 5.7 trillion miles in 365 days! The size of our galaxy in miles is a staggering 5.7 trillion times 100,000, and it is estimated to contain 200 billion stars, 50 percent of which (100 billion) possess solar systems like our own. The next closest galaxy is Andromeda, a galaxy much like our own Milky Way, that is approximately 2.2 million light years away from us. Furthermore, our best telescopes can probe outward into space to a distance of approximately 5 billion light years and view about 500 million galaxies, each of which possesses billions of stars. And these galaxies are only the ones we can detect with the present state of our technology. Truly, the observation made by Enoch the seer is one of the grandest *understatements* of all time: "And were it possible that man could number the particles of the earth, yea, millions of earths like this, it would not be a beginning to the number of thy creations; and thy curtains are stretched out still" (Moses 7:30).

The Savior redeems all that he creates. Such are the sweeping and incomprehensible powers of Jesus, the Victor of Gethsemane. And what's more, these creations are maintained and renewed continually by the very same power possessed by their creator, for

he that ascended up on high, as also he descended below all things, in that he comprehended all things, that he might be in all and through all things, the light of truth;

Which truth shineth. This is the light of Christ . . .

Which light proceedeth forth from the presence of God to fill the immensity of space—

The light which is in all things, which giveth life to all things, which is the law by which all things are governed, even the power of God who sitteth upon his

15

throne, who is in the bosom of eternity, who is in the midst of all things. (D&C 88:6–13)

## THE ATONEMENT AND THE BITTER CUP

All that the Atonement was and is, all that it put into effect or operation, all that it set in motion, all that it touches in the vastness of space for time and eternity centers on a moment in this earth's temporal history at the spot called Gethsemane. It is true that the Atonement involved both Gethsemane and Golgotha, but the agony of redemption began in Gethsemane. Prophets have taught that the Savior's greatest suffering was in Gethsemane. President Joseph Fielding Smith said:

> [Christ's] greatest suffering was in Gethsemane. We speak of the passion of Jesus Christ. A great many people have an idea that when he was on the cross, and nails were driven into his hands and feet, that was his great suffering. His great suffering was before he ever was placed upon the cross. It was in the Garden of Gethsemane that the blood oozed from the pores of his body: "Which suffering caused myself, even God, the greatest of all, to tremble because of pain, and to bleed at every pore, and to suffer both body and spirit—and would that I might not drink the bitter cup, and shrink."
>
> That was not when he was on the cross; that was in the garden. That is where he bled from every pore in his body. Now I cannot comprehend that pain. (*Doctrines of Salvation*, 1:130)

And so it was that by divine decree and ordination, all laws were poised for this greatest of events we sometimes refer to simply as Gethsemane. All things pointed to it. God the Father's great plan of happiness was created around it. It was the Father's will that such a thing take place. Jesus was the perfectly innocent but willing volunteer. And thereby hangs the tale, for the Savior consistently and repeatedly in scripture referred to the events in Gethsemane as "the bitter cup."

To every disciple of every dispensation, Gethsemane was and is the sweetest of victories: "From the terrible conflict in Gethsemane, Christ emerged a victor" (Talmage, *Jesus the Christ*, 614). That victory means everything to us as mortals. Because of it, every human being who seeks God's love receives not only that love but hope as well. Yet, to the Sinless One himself, a being of infinite goodness and perfect sensitivity, Gethsemane was the ultimate torture, the darkest hour, the starkest terror. His most extreme distress had little to do with the thought of physical death, even the hideous kind of death brought on by crucifixion. Rather, to that one being in all the universe who was personally and completely undeserving of the horrible, infinite punishments inflicted, Gethsemane was the bitterest anguish, the greatest contradiction, the gravest injustice, the bitterest of cups to drink. Yet, the will of the Father was that the bitter cup be swallowed—drained to its dregs. And drained it was, swallowed to the last drop by Christ. Thus it would be said, in ultimate irony, that the will of the Son was "swallowed up in the will of the Father" (Mosiah 15:7).

Irony and contradiction are two of the best descriptors of Gethsemane's bitter cup, causing thoughtful disciples to reflect on the nature of tests and trials in mortality and how the lessons of the bitter cup can have profound meaning in their lives. The Prophet Joseph Smith taught that the Savior "descended in suffering below that which man can suffer; or, in other words,

17

suffered greater sufferings, and was exposed to more powerful contradictions than any man can be" (*Lectures on Faith*, 59). Perhaps the greatest trials are those which seem the most unfair, but the faithful may take comfort in knowing that there is One who understands with perfect empathy. In Gethsemane, the contradictions that constitute the bitter cup are seen with crystal clarity. He who was the Son of the Highest descended below all things. He who was sinless was weighed down by the crushing sins of everyone else. He who was the light and the life of the world was surrounded by darkness and death. He who was sent to earth out of love and who was characterized as Love suffered the effects of enmity, or hatred, toward God. He who was the essence of loyalty was the object of betrayal and disloyalty. He who did nothing but good suffered evil. He who was the Righteous One was buffeted by the enemy of all righteousness. And from it all, he emerged victorious.

That Latter-day Saints are different from almost all other Christians in placing so much emphasis on Gethsemane is evidenced in our expanded and expansive canon of scripture. The events of Gethsemane are a focal point of Latter-day Saint scripture, which testifies of its profundity. The experience of the bitter cup seems to have had such an effect on the Savior himself that he discussed it not only in Gethsemane but during his ministry to the Nephites after his resurrection and in his revelations of the latter days. It affected Jesus to the very core of his being. By studying the bitter cup, we can see, really see, how the bitterest agony for One opened the door to the sweetest ecstasy for all.

My young friend Brittany did not know about the doctrine of the bitter cup. But she did know the most important thing of all—Jesus did what he did out of love. She knew of his love for her, and she loved him. On this point she was as articulate and clear as the scriptures she could not read. Jesus endured the suffering of the bitter cup out of love. He endured the bitter cup so that we don't have to. As the apostle John said, "We love him, because he first loved us" (1 John 4:19). By studying the bitter cup, we can have a guide and support to help make sense of life's trials, sorrows, suffering, and contradictions. We can know of a surety that God's love is as deep and profound as the Savior's suffering. We can learn the precious price of redemption.

And when the hour was come, he sat down, and the twelve apostles with him.

And he said unto them, With desire I have desired to eat this passover with you before I suffer. . . .

And he took bread, and gave thanks, and brake it, and gave unto them, saying, This is my body which is given for you: this do in remembrance of me.

Like wise also the cup after supper, saying, This cup is the new testament in my blood, which is shed for you.

LUKE 22:14–20

When Jesus had spoken these words, he went forth with his disciples over the brook Cedron, where was a garden, into the which he entered, and his disciples.

And Judas also, which betrayed him, knew the place: for Jesus oft-times resorted thither with his disciples.

JOHN 18:1–2

# CHAPTER 2

# The Preparation for the Bitter Cup

The Savior's preparation for the awful events of Gethsemane began to take shape several months before his actual experience in the garden, as he tried to fortify his apostles against the coming suffering and rejection he knew he would have to endure at Jerusalem. The authors of all three Synoptic Gospels (Matthew, Mark, and Luke) indicate that immediately after his experience on the Mount of Transfiguration with Peter, James, and John, the Savior began to teach his disciples about his impending death. Matthew says: "From that time forth began Jesus to shew unto his disciples, how that he must go unto Jerusalem, and suffer many things of the elders and chief priests and scribes, and be killed, and be raised again the third day" (Matthew 16:21). Mark points out the rejection of Jesus as a separate aspect of his suffering: "And he began to teach them, that the Son of man must suffer many things, *and* be rejected of the elders, and of the chief priests, and scribes" (Mark 8:31; emphasis added).

## REJECTION OF JESUS

The rejection Jesus experienced his whole life, but which intensified as he neared the end, actually centered in his own family long before the last six months of his ministry. John records, "Neither did his brethren believe in him" (John 7:5). His "brethren," or half brothers James, Joses, Simon, and Judas (Matthew 13:55) chided and goaded him over his messianic claims, undoubtedly seeking to mock and chastise him (John 7:2–4, 7). Thus it may be said, colloquially but fairly, that Jesus himself, the great Jehovah come to earth, was the product of a part-member family, thereby showing his followers that not even he was exempt from the heartache and rejection sometimes inflicted by those whom we most wish could be our greatest supporters.

How this must have stung! In the Savior's case, this suffering and rejection from family members was but a prelude to even greater and more intense anguish he had to endure at the end of his life. It demonstrates that the prophecies uttered by Isaiah began to be fulfilled in a most exacting and all-encompassing manner long before the culminating events of Gethsemane. Truly, in every way Jesus was "despised and rejected of men; a man of sorrows, and acquainted with grief" (Isaiah 53:3). Thus, his disciples in our day may take comfort in knowing that because of his own experience, Jesus comprehends every kind of pain, sorrow, and rejection. He therefore is able to be both a perfect advocate and a perfect nurturer for those who suffer, even those who suffer deep pain from the actions and cruelty of others through no fault of their own.

However great they were, the apostles of ancient times little understood what Jesus was telling them about his suffering (current and impending) as well as his approaching and inevitable redemptive sacrifice. In fact, President Wilford Woodruff said that the apostles of the meridian dispensation had as little idea that Jesus was going to suffer death and be taken from them as had the early apostles of our own dispensation that Joseph Smith was going to suffer a martyr's fate. He said: "I remember very well the last charge that Joseph gave to the Apostles. We had as little idea that he was going from us as the Apostles of the Savior did that He was going to be taken from them. Joseph talked with us as plainly as did the Savior to His Apostles, but we did not understand that he was about to depart from us any more than the Apostles understood the Savior" (*Collected Discourses*, 188).

Reasons for their failing to understand are undoubtedly complex, but Jesus' rebuke of Peter for "savour[ing] not the things that be of God, but the things that be of men" (Mark 8:33) may indicate that the apostles were expecting that, in the end, Jesus would be the same kind of Messiah the rest of the Jewish people were looking for: a towering military conqueror and political deliverer.

As the Savior's mortal life moved unalterably closer to the final week when his prophesied and nearly unbearable suffering would explode upon him, his fame spread, his popularity waxed and waned, opposition toward him increased among Jewish leaders, and plots to take his life fomented beneath the surface of a society whose leaders contemptuously conspired against him. On the last Sunday of his mortal existence, the Savior made his triumphal entry into Jerusalem, just as the long awaited King-Messiah was expected to do and as other kings of Israel had done (1 Kings 1:38–39). He rode upon a donkey, symbolic of royalty and in fulfillment of prophecy (Matthew

21:4–5), rather than upon a horse, symbolic of war and conquest. In ironic fulfillment of Jewish messianic expectation, when Jesus comes again he will be riding a white horse as the ultimate conqueror of all—only this will be his great and terrible second coming (Revelation 19:11–16).

Messianic fervor and expectation reached a feverish pitch as Jesus made his triumphal entry into Jerusalem the last Sunday of his mortal existence. Matthew testified of this when he reported that

> a very great multitude spread their garments in the way; others cut down branches from the trees, and strawed them in the way.
>
> And the multitudes that went before, and that followed, cried, saying, Hosanna to the Son of David: Blessed is he that cometh in the name of the Lord; Hosanna in the highest.
>
> And when he was come into Jerusalem, *all the city was moved*, saying, Who is this?
>
> And the multitude said, This is Jesus the prophet of Nazareth of Galilee. (Matthew 21:8–11; emphasis added)

It is likely that some were expecting Jesus, as the long-awaited King-Messiah-Deliverer-Conqueror, to enter the Jerusalem Temple via the Eastern, or Golden, Gate, turn toward the Antonia Fortress, drive the Roman overlords from the land of Israel, and, in fulfillment of Davidic expectation, establish an idyllic messianic kingdom, much as King David had done when he conquered Jerusalem in 1004 B.C. and set up an unrivaled domain (2 Samuel 5:6–10). Jesus did enter the Temple complex, but instead of going to the Antonia Fortress where Roman

sentries were barracked, he went to the Temple courtyard and drove out the money changers. This action dashed the hopes of those who thought their political deliverer-warrior had actually come, and it further angered Jewish leaders, who began looking in earnest for a way to rid themselves of the prophet from Nazareth, who was disrupting the flow of economic traffic at the center of Jewish life—the Temple (Matthew 21:15). The apostle John summarizes the attitude of two groups of leaders, the chief priests and the Pharisees, who were, strangely enough, at that moment in alignment over Jesus: "If we let him thus alone, all men will believe on him: and the Romans shall come and take away both our place and our nation" (John 11:48). Elements of Jewish leadership from all quarters of society, even those from opposite ends of the political-religious spectrum, were now irreversibly set against the Savior. His fate was sealed.

## THE PASSOVER PLOT COMPLETED

So it was that a couple of days after his triumphal entry, and two days before the Passover celebration, perhaps Tuesday of the last week of the Savior's mortal life, Luke tells of the Passover conspiracy being completed:

> Now the feast of unleavened bread drew nigh, which is called the Passover.
>
> And the chief priests and scribes sought how they might kill him; for they feared the people.
>
> Then entered Satan into Judas surnamed Iscariot, being of the number of the twelve.
>
> And he went his way, and communed with the chief priests and captains, how he might betray him unto them.

And they were glad, and covenanted to give him money.

And he promised, and sought opportunity to betray him unto them in the absence of the multitude. (Luke 22:1–6)

A more chilling description than this one can hardly be imagined. Luke tells of Satan entering "into Judas surnamed Iscariot" (Luke 22:3) and the latter covenanting and promising to betray the Master in the absence of the multitude. We might be tempted to ascribe Luke's description to hyperbole except that John (whose Gospel is not one of the Synoptic Gospels and is therefore a good source of corroboration) also tells us that Satan entered into Judas during the evening of the Last Supper (John 13:27).

At this point, we might ask if such a thing is really possible. Could Satan really have entered Judas, a member of the Twelve? "Perhaps," wrote Elder Bruce R. McConkie, "for Satan is a spirit man, a being who was born the offspring of God in pre-existence, and who was cast out of heaven for rebellion. He and his followers have power in some cases to enter the [physical] bodies of men" (*Doctrinal New Testament Commentary*, 1:701–2).

Though such a circumstance is almost too terrifying to contemplate, we have the assurance of a modern prophet that Satan can have no power over a person unless he is granted it by the individual: "All beings who have bodies have power over those who have not. The devil has no power over us only as we permit him" (Smith, *Teachings of the Prophet Joseph Smith*, 181).

Whether or not Satan literally entered into Judas on this occasion, Judas "had sold himself to the devil" well before he

sold Jesus into the hands of evil men (Talmage, *Jesus the Christ*, 592). The agreed-upon price of betrayal was thirty pieces of silver, which was the price of a slave in Jesus' day, as foreseen in prophecy (Exodus 21:28–32; Zechariah 11:12). The chief priests with whom Judas communicated were those very leaders who later actively "sought for witness against Jesus to put him to death" (Mark 14:55) and incited the multitudes to reject their King (John 19:6, 15). It appears that the "captains" whom Luke describes as covenanting with Judas (Luke 22:4) were officers of the temple guard, chosen mostly from the Levites. They were also with the chief priests shouting, "Crucify him, crucify him" when Jesus was arraigned before the Roman governor, Pontius Pilate (John 19:6).

## THE PASSOVER MEAL

After Judas' preparations had been completed and the plot was in place, the Savior's own preparation for Gethsemane culminated in the "cup after supper," the sacrament, which involved the ordinance of the washing of the feet. That is, before Jesus endured the "bitter cup," as he himself called his experience in Gethsemane, he fortified himself and his apostles against the coming spiritual onslaught by instituting the sacrament of the Lord's Supper only hours before the fury in Gethsemane was unleashed.

The sacrament itself required some preparation, for it had been celebrated the previous twelve hundred years or so as the traditional Passover, or Seder, meal of the people of Israel. The Hebrew word *seder* means "order, or arrangement" and evokes images of elaborate preparation of special foods to be eaten in a prescribed order as well as specific teachings and scriptures to be recited in proper sequence throughout the evening.

Passover commemorated the night in Egypt when the angel of death, sent by Jehovah, passed over the homes of the children of Israel and spared the lives of their firstborn, providing they had sacrificed an unblemished male lamb, eaten the roasted meat, and daubed the blood of the lamb on the lintel and doorposts of their houses (Exodus 12:5, 7, 13, 22–23, 27).

It was a night of judgment, but the substitutionary death of the Passover lamb brought forgiveness to God's people, Israel. It washed away 430 years of Egypt's contamination. The blood of the lamb protected them from the wrath of the Almighty. Its roasted flesh nourished their bodies with strength for the long, perilous journey ahead. They ate in haste, loins girded, staff in hand, shoes on their feet, prepared to leave at any moment at God's command. In that awe-filled night of waiting, they experienced Jehovah's loving protection, even in the midst of the unleashing of His fierce judgment. (Rosen and Rosen, *Christ in the Passover*, 23–24)

The English word *Passover* is a translation of the Hebrew *pesach*, which means "to skip over, to hop" and also carries the connotation of "protecting." *Passover* can be used to mean either the sacrificial ceremony or the actual lamb itself, as in Luke 22:7: "Then came the day of unleavened bread, when *the passover* must be killed" (emphasis added).

The Greek equivalent of *pesach* is *pascha*, hence the term "paschal lamb," which was sacrificed as part of the annual Passover ceremony so that Israel would always remember the Lord's power and protection. The meaning of the practice has been summarized in the following way: "The slain lamb, the sheltering behind its blood and the eating of its flesh, constituted the *pesach*, the protection of God's chosen people beneath the sheltering wings of the Almighty. . . . It was not merely that the Lord passed by the houses of the Israelites, but that He stood on guard, *protecting* each blood-sprinkled door! [The Lord . . . will not suffer the destroyer to come in (Exodus 12:23b)]" (Rosen and Rosen, *Christ in the Passover*, 22–23).

During Jesus' time, the Passover lambs used in the feast were killed on the fourteenth day of the month of Nissan, and the meal was eaten between sundown and midnight, in conformity with Exodus 12:6. Because the Jewish day began at sundown, the Passover feast itself took place on the fifteenth of Nissan. The Feast of Unleavened Bread followed the Passover feast and lasted seven more days (Exodus 12:15–20; 23:15; 34:18; Deuteronomy 16:1–8).

The special foods and other items of the first Passover, as well as their arrangement, were highly symbolic, although most Jewish people today do not recognize or acknowledge the Christ-centered symbolism of those elements. The following is a summary of the most important elements of the first Passover:

1. Just as "the firstborn in the land of Egypt [would] die" (Exodus 11:5), so Jesus, the Firstborn of the Father (D&C 93:21), would die.

2. Just as the Passover sacrifice was a male lamb "without blemish" (Exodus 12:5), so Jesus was "as of a lamb without blemish" (1 Peter 1:19) and was called the Lamb of God (1 Nephi 11:21).

3. Just as no bone of the Passover lamb was to be broken

# THE PASSOVER THROUGH THE AGES

| The Original Passover in the Time of Moses | The Traditional Passover at the Time of Christ | The Jewish Passover as Practiced Today |
|---|---|---|
| *EXODUS 12* | *THE SEDER (Luke 22)* | *THE SEDER Today* |
| 1. A MALE LAMB<br>• Slain as a sacrifice<br>• Blood on doorpost<br>• Lamb eaten | 1. A MALE LAMB<br>• Slain at temple altar<br>• Blood on doorpost<br>• Lamb eaten | 1. SHANK BONE of a lamb |
| 2. UNLEAVENED BREAD<br>• At the meal and for 7 more days<br>• Symbolized haste in leaving Egypt | 2. UNLEAVENED BREAD | 2. UNLEAVENED BREAD (matzos) |
| 3. BITTER HERBS<br>Symbolized the bitterness of bondage in Egypt | 3. BITTER HERBS | 3. HORSERADISH (bitter herb) |
| | 4. FOUR CUPS OF WINE<br>• Cup of blessing (telling of the story)<br>• Cup before eating (eating of the food)<br>• Cup after supper (songs of thanks)<br>• Cup of Elijah | 4. FOUR CUPS OF WINE |
| | 5. OTHER FOODS FOR FEAST | 5. PARSLEY (spring) |
| | | 6. SALT WATER (Red Sea) |
| | | 7. AN EGG (new life) |
| | | 8. "HAROSET"–reddish fruit salad (representing brick mortar) |
| | | 9. MEAL–main course of turkey, chicken, etc. |
| | | 10. GEFILTE FISH |
| Note what the sacrificial lamb symbolized. | Note what elements of the Passover Jesus gave as a new way to remember him. | Note how modern Passover services omit the symbolism of the Messiah. |
| *Future sacrifice of Jesus Christ* | *Bread and wine* (cup after supper; Luke 22:19–20) | *There is NO LAMB* |

(Exodus 12:46), so no bone of Jesus was broken during his atoning sacrifice (John 19:36).

4.  Just as no stranger was to eat of the Passover lamb (Exodus 12:43), so, too, no stranger (one who is estranged from God through unworthiness) is to eat of the emblems of the sacrifice of the Lamb of God—the sacrament (3 Nephi 18:28–30).

5.  Just as hyssop was associated with the Passover sacrifice (Exodus 12:22), so hyssop was associated with the crucifixion of the great and last sacrifice of the Lamb of God (John 19:29).

6.  Just as the blood of the Passover lamb caused death to pass by the believers (Exodus 12:13), so the blood of the Lamb of God causes the effects of sin or spiritual death to pass by the believers (John 1:29; Alma 7:14; 11:40–43).

The special foods to be prepared and eaten for the Passover meal changed over the twelve hundred years between the original Passover in Moses' day (Exodus 12–13) and the Passover meal at the time of Jesus. Nevertheless, the three most important elements in Jesus' day continued to be the unleavened bread, the wine, and the male lamb without blemish or spot.

This information, summarized on the accompanying chart, is valuable for several reasons. First, it helps us understand the unstated historical and cultural background that Jesus and his apostles, all of them observant Jews, brought to the last Passover of Jesus' mortal life. It helps us see meaning in the absence of a lamb in the modern observances: the Jewish people lack a knowledge of their Redeemer, the Messiah who has come and gone but will return. Most important, it helps us recognize a connection between the Passover meal and the sacrament of the Lord's Supper. We see what elements of the Passover meal Jesus emphasized in order to help us remember him: the bread and the wine (water).

A significant but sometimes overlooked doctrinal principle is involved here as well. Just as the Atonement itself had been foreshadowed before the coming of Jesus Christ in the flesh, so too the sacrament had been foreshadowed as early as Melchizedek's and Abraham's day. We remember that Abraham had made a covenant with God, the terms of which included the promises of land, posterity, priesthood, and salvation through the Messiah. Abraham's spiritual leader was Melchizedek, the very same man who was translated because of his righteousness and his work in pointing his people to the coming of Jesus Christ through participation in the ordinances of God (JST Genesis 14:25–36; Alma 13:14–19). Thus, after Abraham's return from war with the kings, the following scene unfolded: "And Melchizedek, king of Salem, brought forth bread and wine; and he break bread and blest it; and he blest the wine, he being the priest of the most high God, and he gave to Abram, and he blessed him, and said, Blessed Abram, thou art a man of the most high God, possessor of heaven and of earth" (JST Genesis 14:17–18).

The Joseph Smith Translation makes it clear that the bread and wine were more than just a snack after a hard day on the battlefield—a point lost in other versions of the Bible. Melchizedek broke the bread and blessed it and blessed the wine precisely *because* he was the priest of the Most High God and had the authority to administer the ordinances of God. We are further convinced by Elder Bruce R. McConkie's observation that the ordinance of the sacrament was purposely foreshadowed and prefigured "some two thousand years before its formal institution among men, when 'Melchizedek, king of Salem, brought forth bread and wine; and he brake bread and blest it, and he blest wine, he being priest of the most high God.' . . . It will be administered after the Lord comes again, to all the faithful of all ages, as they in resurrected glory assemble before him" (*Promised Messiah*, 384).

## IN THE UPPER ROOM

We know that the Savior was aware of the need to prepare for the Passover feast because on the day when the Passover lamb was traditionally killed, he sent the apostles Peter and John to the home of someone who was himself a disciple so that they could make the necessary preparations. We know the man to whom the apostles were sent was a disciple of Jesus because Jesus told the apostles to tell the homeowner that the Master was requesting the use of his furnished upper room (Luke 22:7–12). That is, Jesus was the homeowner's Master as well.

On the afternoon of the appointed day when the Passover lambs were to be killed, while Jesus and his apostles were making their preparations for the Passover feast, thousands of paschal lambs were being slain within the precincts of the Jerusalem temple by representatives of families getting ready to participate in their own Passover feasts. A portion of blood from each of the Passover lambs was sprinkled at the foot of the great altar by one of a large number of priests on duty for the occasion. The Jewish historian Josephus indicates that the lambs had to be slain between the ninth and eleventh hours of the day, that is, between 3 and 5 P.M. Some authorities hold that during the time of Jesus, two nights were devoted to the Passover observance and the lamb could be eaten during either of the two days. This accommodation was made because the greatly increased population in Jerusalem during Passover seasons of the meridian dispensation necessitated the ceremonial slaughtering of more lambs than could be sacrificed on a single day (Talmage, *Jesus the Christ*, 618). According to Josephus, the number of Passover lambs slain at a single Passover season during this period was 256,500 (*Wars*, 6.9:3).

With preparations completed, Jesus sat down with his apostles in the upper room of one of Jerusalem's more expensive houses to participate in the last Passover of his mortal life. What emotion must have choked the atmosphere of this significant occasion as Jesus said to the assembled group, "With desire I have desired to eat this passover with you before I suffer" (Luke 22:15). Or, as the New International Version of the Bible translates this passage, "I have eagerly desired to eat this Passover with you before I suffer" (Luke 22:15). The very Being who instituted the first Passover more than twelve hundred years before now expressed his yearning to be with his closest friends to show them how everything about the Passover pointed to himself.

We have every reason to believe that the Seder meal on this special night followed the traditional manner of presentation—up to a point. Though the critical, most significant elements of the Passover had been revealed by Jehovah in Old Testament times, by the time of Christ some elements had been borrowed from Roman custom. One of these was the kind of table used. Called a *triclinium*, this table was low to the floor and composed of three sections configured in a U shape. Both the table and the room in which it was set were called the triclinium. Known from historical texts, actual specimens of tricliniums have been found in modern times through archaeological excavation in the Holy Land at Herodium, Nablus, Sepphoris, and the modern Jewish Quarter of the Old City of Jerusalem.

Rabbinic and New Testament sources tell us that diners reclined around the table, resting on their left elbows, heads toward the table, feet pointed away, reaching and eating with their right hands, which were free. This form of dining imitated the practice of the free, wealthy, and aristocratic members of Roman Hellenistic society. According to Jewish tradition, all who participate in the Passover are regarded as kings before God during this special time, which celebrates liberty and protection of the once oppressed.

The seat on the outside edge of the triclinium, second in from the end, was reserved for special guests, dignitaries, or learned teachers. It is possible that Jesus sat here as he led the Passover service. The Gospel of John helps us further visualize the seating arrangements at the triclinium, specifically, who was seated in front of, or to the right side of, Jesus. "Now there was leaning on Jesus' bosom one of his disciples, whom Jesus loved" (John 13:23). That is, as Jesus reclined with feet away from the table, John (the "beloved" disciple) was situated so he could lean back and rest his head and shoulder against the chest of Jesus.

## THE NEW ORDINANCE INSTITUTED

The order of events probably unfolded according to recognized custom. The first cup of wine was blessed and drunk. Hands were washed as a blessing was recited. Bitter herbs, symbolic of the bitterness of Egyptian bondage, were eaten—dipped in sour broth made of vinegar and bruised fruit, both messianic symbols. Because of the composition of the group (there being no youngest son to ask questions about why this night was different from all other nights), the origins of Passover were likely recounted by the leader of the Seder service—who was, in this instance, Jesus. The lamb was then placed on the table or, if already on the table, it was acknowledged, and the first parts of the Hallel (Psalms 113 and 114) were sung. The second cup of wine was blessed and drunk.

But then something extraordinary happened. According to the Gospel of Luke, instead of breaking the unleavened bread of Passover and reciting the traditional blessing appropriate at this juncture, Jesus "took bread, and gave thanks, and brake it, and gave unto them, saying, This is my body which is given for you: this do in remembrance of me" (Luke 22:19). The disciples must have sat in stunned silence as they struggled to eat a piece of the bread and then consume a fragment of the lamb, as was the custom. Such a thing as this had never been done before. Such a comment as Jesus had made would have been totally inappropriate—unless, of course, the commentator really was the Messiah.

From this point, a typical Passover dinner usually proceeded at a leisurely pace until everything was eaten and the atmosphere of celebration increased. But the apostles of the Lamb had just eaten a piece of bread and a fragment of lamb, not in remembrance of the events of the first Passover (Exodus 12:8) but in remembrance of the Bread of Life and the Lamb of God, just as Jesus had intimated they would when he had delivered his Bread of Life discourse months earlier. It seems likely that the apostles would have remembered at that moment in the upper room the words Jesus had uttered on the earlier occasion. That event had been momentous not only because it immediately followed the miracle of the loaves and fishes in feeding the

five thousand but also because the words Jesus spoke were themselves so unusual, even astonishing:

> I am that bread of life.
>
> Your fathers did eat manna in the wilderness, and
> are dead.
>
> This is the bread which cometh down from heaven,
> that a man may eat thereof, and not die.
>
> I am the living bread which came down from
> heaven: if any man eat of this bread, he shall live for
> ever: and the bread that I will give is my flesh, which I
> will give for the life of the world.
>
> The Jews therefore strove among themselves, saying,
> How can this man give us [his] flesh to eat?
>
> Then Jesus said unto them, Verily, verily, I say unto
> you, Except ye eat the flesh of the Son of man, and
> drink his blood, ye have no life in you.
>
> Whoso eateth my flesh, and drinketh my blood,
> hath eternal life; and I will raise him up at the last day.
> (John 6:48–54)

Now, on this night of nights, the apostles were actually
doing in symbolic fashion the very thing Jesus had described—
eating the lamb, both literally and symbolically. But more sur-
prises were yet to come. As is still well known in modern times,
ordinarily after the dinner portion of the Seder celebration has
been completed, the third cup of wine, the "cup after supper"—
what the rabbis also called "the cup of blessing"—was mixed
with water, and then blessed and drunk, again in an atmosphere
of celebration. The Gospel of Luke, however, describes the
scene in the upper room with solemn brevity and poignancy:

"Likewise also the cup after supper, saying, This cup is the new testament in my blood, which is shed for you" (Luke 22:20).

Though the apostles would not fully appreciate the symbolism of mixing water with the third cup of wine until after the crucifixion, when the Savior's pierced side yielded blood *and water* (John 19:34–35), they could not have mistaken the revolutionary change that had been enacted during their time together that night in what had started out as a traditional Passover celebration. Nor could they have missed much of its meaning and significance. The ordinance of Passover now centered squarely on Jesus of Nazareth. Instead of remembering the Exodus from Egypt, a slaughtered pastoral animal (the lamb), and escape from the physical and mental bondage of slavery, now and forever more, followers of Jesus were to remember him who established the Passover, remember him who was the true king over the children of Israel, remember him who was the lamb slain from before the foundations of the world, remember him who saves from all types of bondage—physical, mental, emotional and spiritual—indeed, remember him always. In what is probably the earliest recorded account of the events of the Last Supper we read: "For as often as ye eat this bread, and drink this cup, ye do shew the Lord's death till he come" (1 Corinthians 11:26, which is perhaps the apostle Paul's earliest letter).

The new ordinance now known as the sacrament replaced the old system of animal sacrifice in which a priest ritually slaughtered an offering on behalf of the covenantor. The sacrament of the Lord's Supper raised to a new height the level and intensity of individual commitment and interaction with God. Instead of communal involvement and interaction with a priest at the Temple in Jerusalem, it demanded a more direct and intimate communion with Deity. It did away with any priestly intermediary as well as almost all outward aspects of the old system of blood sacrifice. What the Savior said explicitly to the Nephites he said by inference to the apostles during the Last Supper: "And ye shall offer up unto me no more the shedding of blood; yea, your sacrifices and your burnt offerings shall be done away, for I will accept none of your sacrifices and your burnt offerings. And ye shall offer for a sacrifice unto me a broken heart and a contrite spirit" (3 Nephi 9:19–20).

These verses are connected to both the sacrament and Gethsemane in a startling way. The same two aspects of sacrifice that the Lord commanded the Nephites to offer in place of animals are the same two aspects of sacrifice he asks each of us to offer. And these two offerings we are required to make as we partake of the sacrament are the very things Jesus, the Lamb of God, experienced during his agony in the Garden of Gethsemane and on the cross at the moment he died: Jesus experienced a contrite ("crushed") spirit in the garden and a broken heart on the cross. For each of us, the broken heart and contrite spirit lead to newness of life through repentance. President J. Reuben Clark Jr., a counselor in the First Presidency, said, "Under the new covenant that came in with Christ, the sinner must offer the sacrifice out of his own life, not by offering the blood of some other creature; he must give up his sins, he must repent, he himself must make the sacrifice . . . so that he would become a better and changed man" (*Behold the Lamb of God*, 107–8).

Truly, the "cup after supper," which was transformed into the sacrament of the Lord's Supper, was important preparation for the "bitter cup" of which the Savior partook. It serves as our tangible link with the Savior as well as with the historical events in the upper room, in the Garden of Gethsemane, and on the cross.

The cup after supper fortified the Savior spiritually and emotionally to face burdens and agonies such as no other being will ever bear. It satisfied his yearning to share the true significance of the Passover with the original Twelve, and it provides all disciples everywhere with physical emblems by which to remember him and his atonement. Jesus could go to Gethsemane knowing he had done all to prepare the Twelve to face their own special burdens brought on by the bitter cup that only he would consume but which they would also have to partake of in certain ways. The cup after supper prepared the disciples for future events by providing them one last, profound witness that Jesus was not only the Messiah but the very God who had instituted the Passover more than twelve hundred years before.

## THE LAST SUPPER ENDS

If the activities of the evening had concluded with only the establishment of the sacrament, the night would still have been far spent. It would have left the apostles emotionally and physically drained, not to mention mentally awash in a sea of new and profound ideas, as they tried to internalize the monumental happenings of the evening as well as the monumental feelings that accompanied those events. But, as it turned out, the evening was far from over.

Actually, it was not then nor is it now uncommon for serious-minded, observant Jews to linger around the Passover table for hours singing and discussing the Passover. This night, however, as Jesus and his apostles remained together after the meal, another powerful ordinance was instituted by the Savior—the washing of the feet—and many powerful and important teachings were also delivered by the Master. Jesus concluded his final teaching moments on this night of nights by offering what has come to be known as the great high priestly prayer, or the great intercessory prayer. All of these key events after the Last Supper, along with their accompanying doctrines and concepts, are uniquely recorded in the New Testament by John for the benefit of Church members in these latter days (John 13–17). In fact, we could make a good case that John was really writing for seasoned and valiant members of the Lord's true Church. This truth becomes apparent when we consider the uniqueness of John's expressions in both his Gospel and his Apocalypse (the book of Revelation). It is particularly significant that John speaks of Jesus' instruction about the Second Comforter (John 14:16–23; Smith, *Teachings of the Prophet Joseph Smith*, 150), the nature of eternal life as knowing personally God and his Son Jesus Christ (John 17:3; D&C 132:24), and the Savior's work to make "us kings and priests unto God and his Father" (Revelation 1:6).

Jesus instituted the ordinance of the washing of the feet as "a holy and sacred rite, one performed by the saints in the seclusion of their temple sanctuaries," according to Elder Bruce R. McConkie (*Doctrinal New Testament Commentary*, 1:708). It appears to be an ordinance of ultimate approbation by the Lord and, in a fascinating way, stands in direct contrast to the ordinance of the dusting off of the feet, which seems to be the ultimate earthly ordinance of condemnation by the Lord, performed only by his authorized servants.

That Jesus performed the ordinance of the washing of the feet for his closest friends is another indication of his attempts to prepare them for the coming spiritual onslaught in Gethsemane as well as to teach them further about his role in fulfilling of the law of Moses. As the Joseph Smith Translation summarizes, "He that has washed his hands and his head, needeth not save to wash his feet, but is clean every whit; and ye are clean, but not all. Now this was the custom of the Jews under their law; wherefore, Jesus did this that the law might be fulfilled" (JST John 13:10).

John's Gospel further tells us that after the washing of the feet, Jesus said to his apostles: "Now is the Son of man glorified, and God is glorified in him. If God be glorified in him, God shall also glorify him in himself, and shall straightway glorify him. Little children, yet a little while I am with you. Ye shall seek me: and as I said unto the Jews, Whither I go, ye cannot come. . . . Simon Peter said unto him, Lord, whither goest thou? Jesus answered him, Whither I go, thou canst not follow me now; but thou shalt follow me afterwards" (John 13:31–36).

Here Jesus speaks as though his looming agony in Gethsemane and the suffering on the cross are a foregone conclusion and his glorification of the Father already a living reality. Thus, where he is about to go and what he is about to accomplish have already been foreseen by himself and his Father. The apostles cannot yet follow him, but they soon will, even in the manner of their own deaths, in some cases. With the perspective afforded by hindsight, this prophecy clearly appears to be an important foreshadowing directed to Peter: "Whither I go, thou canst not follow me now; but thou shalt follow me afterwards." According to tradition, Peter was later crucified head downward for the cause of his Master because he felt unworthy to die in the exact manner of the Lord (Eusebius, *Ecclesiastical History* 3.1.2).

## THEY SANG A HYMN

We do not know at what moment Judas left the Passover dinner to consummate his act of betrayal; the four Gospel accounts are not clear on this point (Talmage, *Jesus the Christ*, 619). We only know that he left sometime after the Savior identified him as the betrayer, though that identification was not recognized by all present. Elder James E. Talmage has written: "The others understood the Lord's remark as an instruction to Judas to attend to some duty or go upon some errand of ordinary kind, perhaps to purchase something for the further celebration of the Passover, or to carry gifts to some of the poor, for Judas was the treasurer of the party and 'had the bag.' But Iscariot understood. His heart was all the more hardened by the discovery that Jesus knew of his infamous plans, and he was maddened by the humiliation he felt in the Master's presence" (*Jesus the Christ*, 598).

Moreover, we do not know at what moment Jesus and the apostles left the upper room to proceed to the Garden of Gethsemane. John 14:31 reports Jesus saying to the group after his instruction on the two Comforters, "Arise, let us go hence." Indeed, the opening content of John 15, Jesus' discourse on the True Vine, suggests an outdoor setting because of the readily visible images of vines or vineyards outside Jerusalem's city walls. Others have been less definitive in assigning a location to all the teachings found in John 14, 15, 16, and 17. However we view the sequence of scenes, though, we know that at some point before the end of their Passover experience together, they concluded by singing together. "And when they had sung an hymn, they went out into the mount of Olives" (Mark 14:26). Likely, this hymn was the last part of the great Hallel, that magnificent set of messianic psalms (Psalms 115–18) whose thinly veiled meanings testify of Jesus Christ. Though the Hallel was ordinarily sung as part of the Passover service or dinner, it seems most significant that at this most solemn and eventful moment in the Lord's mortal ministry, he and his anointed servants concluded their time together by singing a sacred hymn. On this point, Elder Boyd K. Packer has commented: "There are many references in the scriptures, both ancient and modern, that attest to the influence of righteous music. The Lord, Himself, was prepared for His greatest test through its influence, for the scripture records: 'And when they had sung an hymn, they went out into the mount of Olives.' (Mark 14:26.)" (*Ensign*, January 1974, 25).

I have been in meetings when hymns have lifted, blessed, built, and taught the worshipers more than anything else could have. A few years ago, I sat in a sacrament meeting in a room overlooking the Old City of Jerusalem. I had been privileged to take in that scene many times before, but on this Sabbath day the sacrament hymn was "O Savior, Thou Who Wearest a Crown." The moment we began singing, something struck me powerfully—the words, the scene before me, the spiritual power of the Atonement itself, or perhaps, a combination of all of these. Against the backdrop of the very place where the last hours and acts of the Savior's life unfolded, we sang these lyrics:

> O Savior, thou who wearest
> A crown of piercing thorn,
> The pain thou meekly bearest,
> Weigh'd down by grief and scorn.
> The soldiers mock and flail thee;
> For drink they give thee gall;
> Upon the cross they nail thee
> To die, O King of all.
>
> No creature is so lowly,
> No sinner so depraved,
> But feels thy presence holy

And through thy love is saved.
Though craven friends betray thee,
They feel thy love's embrace;
The very foes who slay thee
Have access to thy grace.

(*Hymns*, no. 197)

At that moment I was dumbfounded. I heard nothing else in the meeting for a long time afterward. It had never occurred to me that the words of that hymn were teaching doctrine and articulated the essence of the Atonement: "The very foes who slay thee / Have access to thy grace." This concept changed me forever, capturing as it did the arresting power of Christ's love and his atoning sacrifice. This sacred hymn taught the point of doctrine that is at the heart of our Heavenly Father's plan: Christ "inviteth them *all* to come unto him and partake of his goodness; and he denieth none that come unto him" (2 Nephi 26:33; emphasis added). I realized in that instant that "all" means *all!*

Perhaps, in some similar way, the apostles had a spiritual experience as they sang a hymn and then went out into the Mount of Olives.

## INTO THE GARDEN

John records the arrival of the group at the Garden of Gethsemane as occurring immediately following the great high priestly prayer, when the Savior of the world gave a personal and tender report to his literal Father, our Father in Heaven, about his earthly ministry. "When Jesus had spoken these words, he went forth with his disciples over the brook Cedron, where was a garden, into the which he entered, and his disciples. And

Judas also, which betrayed him, knew the place: for Jesus oft-times resorted thither with his disciples" (John 18:1–2).

The Garden of Gethsemane is on the lower half of the western slope of the Mount of Olives, directly opposite the Temple Mount. In ancient times it was part of an olive vineyard (*vineyard* is preferred over *orchard*). Jesus and his apostles would have reached it by leaving Jerusalem through one of the city gates, descending the slope of the Temple Mount, crossing the little brook in the narrow Kidron Valley, and entering the lower, western end of the garden. Gethsemane was near the Jerusalem cemetery, well used from the tenth century B.C. onward. A full moon would have been shining brightly that evening, owing to the time of the month when Passover occurs each year. It is quite possible, as some have suggested (assuming no cloud cover), that the full moon cast the shadow of the Temple over the garden near the graveyard. Jesus and the apostles thus made their way to Gethsemane in the shadow of the Temple by a place of death. Such a scene could not have done other than serve as a foreboding reminder to the Savior of his impending fate and infuse the atmosphere with increasing gloom.

John 18:1–2 discloses two important details about the Garden of Gethsemane. First, Judas Iscariot, who was not with the apostles because he was with the armed force coming to make the arrest, knew the place. Thus, he would know where to find Jesus at that hour of the night. Second, Judas knew about Gethsemane because Jesus had gone there many times before with the Twelve, as Luke confirms (Luke 22:34). We might speculate that when Jesus was in Judea he went to Gethsemane because it was a place of refuge and reflection for him. It is even possible that he went there often because he knew or sensed that this place would be connected to his most important actions in mortality. In his last general conference address, Elder Bruce R. McConkie commented on Gethsemane's significance for Jesus and the disciples:

> Two thousand years ago, outside Jerusalem's walls, there was a pleasant garden spot, Gethsemane by name, where Jesus and his intimate friends were wont to retire for pondering and prayer.
>
> There Jesus taught his disciples that the doctrines of the kingdom, and all of them communed with Him who is the Father of us all, in whose ministry they were engaged, and on whose errand they served.
>
> This sacred spot, like Eden where Adam dwelt, like Sinai from whence Jehovah gave his laws, like Calvary where the Son of God gave his life a ransom for many, this holy ground is where the Sinless Son of the Everlasting Father took upon himself the sins of all men on condition of repentance. (*Ensign*, May 1985, 9)

With Jesus and his apostles in the Garden of Gethsemane, history was now poised for the very event for which the God of heaven and earth, the Great Jehovah, had come into the world as a mortal. The condescension of God was about to be completely fulfilled. The preparation of the cup after supper was about to give way to the bitter cup. And no one could stop this imminent ordeal except the very Being himself who would later say that this was the ultimate reason for his birth, "To this end was I born, and for this cause came I into the world" (John 18:37).

And they came to a place which was named Gethsemane: and he saith to his disciples, Sit ye here, while I shall pray.

And he taketh with him Peter and James and John, and began to be sore amazed, and to be very heavy;

And saith unto them, My soul is exceeding sorrowful unto death: tarry ye here, and watch.

And he went forward a little, and fell on the ground, and prayed that, if it were possible, the hour might pass from him.

And he said, Abba, Father, all things are possible unto thee; take away this cup from me: nevertheless not what I will, but what thou wilt.

MARK 14:32–36

# CHAPTER 3

# The Shock of the Bitter Cup

The word *Gethsemane*, a combination of the two Hebrew terms *gath* and *shemen*, means "oil press." Situated on the lower half of Olivet, or the Mount of Olives, the Garden of Gethsemane was a lovely area and the site of the production of olive oil in ancient times. The traditionally accepted location of the garden still boasts olive trees that have been reputably dated by Hebrew University botanists to be between eighteen hundred and twenty-three hundred years old. What stories these gnarled and venerable living wonders could tell! When Holy Land tour guides, generally inveterate romantics, try to convince their listeners that some of the trees sheltered Christ—they may be right (*Biblical Archaeologist*, May 1977, 14). That this area has been used for the production of both olive oil and wine is confirmed by the remnants of a very old wine press still visible today in the garden area.

When Jesus and his special witnesses approached the entrance to the garden, Jesus instructed the others to sit and pray so as to "enter not into temptation" (Luke 22:40). Matthew and Mark indicate that he took the chief apostles—

Peter, James, and John, who were the First Presidency of the Church in that day—and went a little farther into the garden. But immediately Jesus began to feel very heavy. Matthew adds that He was "exceeding sorrowful even unto death" (Matthew 26:38), and Mark explicitly states that He felt "sore amazed" (Mark 14:33).

Many of us can readily understand what caused the Savior to feel heavy, weighed down, and so depressed as to think of death. Some have wrestled with the kind of hopelessness that can push a person to the brink of destruction, and thus they can further appreciate the mental and spiritual trauma that afflicted Jesus on this darkest of all nights. In his case, however, the trauma was of a kind and degree that no human being could ever experience. For Jesus was weighed down with the sin, sorrow, and suffering of the entire human family. It was an experience that only a God could withstand and not succumb to death. We might correctly suppose that the sins alone of all humankind would produce in the Savior the feelings described by the Gospel writers. But that is not all there is to it.

## HE BECAME US

To be sure, the Savior's heaviness in Gethsemane was caused by all the sins and all the transgressions committed knowingly by everyone who has ever lived on this earth. But his redemption also included payment for all laws and commandments violated in ignorance. Thus, the Savior suffered in Gethsemane for the most wicked actions of the vilest sinners as well as the unwitting transgressions of the meekest of souls. The spiritual and physical feelings brought about by these transgressions, as well as the full effects of all sins and violent acts ever committed, were literally placed upon the Savior and suffered by him on behalf of those who would repent and *allow* the Savior to be the proxy, or substitute, sufferer for their misdeeds. The apostle Paul taught that God "hath made him [Christ] to be sin for us, who knew no sin; that we might be made the righteousness of God in him" (2 Corinthians 5:21).

In other words, in Gethsemane Jesus became *us*, each one of us, and we became him. Our sins were transferred to Jesus. His perfection was transferred to us. He was a substitute recipient for our pain and punishment. He acted in our place to take the consequences and sorrows of wicked behavior, which each of us deserves, so that we could be free from the devastating effects of sin. The scriptures of the Restoration teach that the Savior took to himself the full force of the punishment deserved by each of us. He suffered God's wrath in our place. Elder Neal A. Maxwell observed that "Jesus always deserved and always had the Father's full approval. But when He took our sins upon Him, of divine necessity required by justice He experienced instead 'the fierceness of the wrath of Almighty God' (D&C 76:107; 88:106)" (*Lord, Increase Our Faith*, 13).

The fierceness of the wrath of Almighty God is a terrifying thing to contemplate. In Gethsemane Jesus took the full force of God's overwhelming and retributory punishment. Justice demanded it, and we, who are sinners, deserve it. According to the rules framing the universe, the full consequences of transgressed laws cannot be dismissed or overlooked. They must be borne by someone—the sinner or the substitute. Jesus was that substitute for all of us who will allow him to be so. Elder Boyd K. Packer testified that "upon Him was the burden of all human transgression, all human guilt. . . . By choice, [Christ] accepted the penalty . . . for brutality, immorality, perversion, and corruption, for addiction, for the killings and torture and terror—

for all of it that ever had been or all that ever would be enacted upon this earth" (*Ensign*, May 1988, 69).

This act of pure grace gave our Savior the right to act as our advocate with the Father and to invoke the law of mercy on our behalf. One of the most powerful scenes in all of scripture allows us to part the curtains of heaven and witness the scene of the Savior's pleadings for us:

> Listen to him who is the advocate with the Father, who is pleading your cause before him—
>
> Saying: Father, behold the sufferings and death of him who did no sin, in whom thou wast well pleased; behold the blood of thy Son which was shed, the blood of him whom thou gavest that thyself might be glorified;
>
> Wherefore, Father, spare these my brethren that believe on my name, that they may come unto me and have everlasting life. (D&C 45:3–5)

## PAIN AND SORROW AHEAD OF SIN

Suffering for our sins was a monumental act of love, an incomprehensible gift unmerited by anything we can do. Lehi taught that the Holy Messiah "offereth himself a sacrifice for sin, . . . [for] there is no flesh that can dwell in the presence of God, save it be through the merits, and mercy, and grace of the Holy Messiah" (2 Nephi 2:7–8). But that is not all.

The scriptures also teach that the Savior's suffering was for far more than our sins alone. The prophet Alma taught clearly that the Savior suffered first and foremost for the sorrow, suffering, and sickness of the Lord's people, as well as for their sins. Thus, the Atonement is far more expansive in its reach and far more comprehensive in its effects than we can possibly fully comprehend. Here are Alma's powerful words:

> And he shall go forth, suffering pains and afflictions and temptations of every kind; and this that the word might be fulfilled which saith he will take upon him the pains and the sicknesses of his people.
>
> And he will take upon him death, that he may loose the bands of death which bind his people; and he will take upon him their infirmities, that his bowels may be filled with mercy, according to the flesh, that he may know according to the flesh how to succor his people according to their infirmities.
>
> Now the Spirit knoweth all things; nevertheless the Son of God suffereth according to the flesh that he might take upon him the sins of his people, that he might blot out their transgressions according to the power of his deliverance; and now behold, this is the testimony which is in me.
>
> Now I say unto you that ye must repent, and be born again; for the Spirit saith if ye are not born again ye cannot inherit the kingdom of heaven; therefore come and be baptized unto repentance, that ye may be washed from your sins, that ye may have faith on the Lamb of God, who taketh away the sins of the world, who is mighty to save and to cleanse from all unrighteousness. (Alma 7:11–14)

The Savior's heaviness in Gethsemane, then, was caused not just by our sins but the weight of all the sickness, sorrow, suffering, injustice, and unfairness that everyone on this earth has ever experienced. He suffered for all the heartaches and sorrows caused by broken homes, marital infidelity, abuse of every kind, children gone astray, disloyalty on the part of trusted friends, crises of health, depression, sickness, pain, lost opportunities, loneliness resulting from the death of a loved one, and psychological scars left by horrible events of which some of us cannot even conceive.

An example or two may illustrate the redemptive power the Savior's suffering in Gethsemane can bring to us. A woman whose husband broke his marriage vows by being unfaithful said, "He broke my heart into a million pieces." But she also said that Jesus' substitutionary suffering helped her and her children work through the unmitigated anguish brought on by the hurtful act of a once-trusted husband and father. The Savior *can* change feelings and bind up broken hearts. Knowing that he has perfect empathy because of his knowledge of our feelings and infirmities is helpful. But knowing he can replace our anguish with feelings of peace—again, because of his substitutionary suffering—is truly miraculous. Another woman, in a similar situation, said with great conviction, "Because of the Savior, I have a place to put the hurt."

Another friend has spoken of her wrestle with "the black hole of depression" that comes when she is expecting a child. Rather than being a time of happiness, this becomes for her a time when energy, emotional stability, spirituality, even a portion of life itself are drained out of her. She is confined to her bed for most of the nine months. She described her mental fog and the dark feelings of hopelessness that come in the face of desiring to do the right things—hold family home evenings, teach her young children the value of prayer and how to pray, have family scripture study, make her home a place of peace rather than of dread and desperation—but ultimately being unable to function, unable to provide a mother's love and guidance. The depression completely overwhelms her. "The thing that helped make a difference this last time," she said, "was realizing that the Savior suffered for these things, suffered for me, paid for the things I didn't do but was supposed to do. The Atonement gave me some glimmer of hope because it made up for my inability to do all the things I knew I needed to do but simply could not do. The Atonement was for me."

Indeed, the Atonement, the Savior's suffering in the Garden of Gethsemane, was undertaken for each one of us, for all of our shortcomings as well as lost opportunities. Gethsemane is not just personal and individual but tailor-made for our differing and changing needs. But that is not all.

## THE WEIGHT OF WORLDS

In Gethsemane Jesus took upon himself not only the sorrows and sins of every person who will ever live on this earth but also all the suffering, sorrows, and sins of every being who will ever live on any of the millions and millions of earths in the vast universe which he helped to create under the direction of our Father in Heaven. The Prophet Joseph Smith bore record of his infinite atoning power:

> That by him, and through him, and of him, the worlds are and were created, and the inhabitants thereof are begotten sons and daughters unto God.
>
> That he came into the world, even Jesus, to be crucified for the world, and to bear the sins of the world, and to sanctify the world, and to cleanse it from all unrighteousness;

That through him all might be saved whom the Father had put into his power and made by him. (D&C 76: 24, 41–42)

We glimpse the magnitude of all those creations that "the Father had put into his power and made by him" by reviewing a few verses the Lord revealed to the ancient prophets Moses and Enoch:

And behold, the glory of the Lord was upon Moses, so that Moses stood in the presence of God, and talked with him face to face. And the Lord God said unto Moses: For mine own purpose have I made these things. Here is wisdom and it remaineth in me. . . .

And worlds without number have I created; and I also created them for mine own purpose; and by the Son I created them, which is mine Only Begotten. (Moses 1:31–33)

And were it possible that man could number the particles of the earth, yea, millions of earths like this, it would not be a beginning to the number of thy creations; and thy curtains are stretched out still; and yet thou art there, and thy bosom is there; and also thou art just; thou art merciful and kind forever. (Moses 7:30)

Thus, the Savior has redeemed through his payment in Gethsemane, and later on the cross, all that he has created. In the same revelation to Enoch that speaks of millions of earths like this one, the Lord indicated why Jesus experienced the Atonement on this earth rather than on one of the millions of other earths: "Wherefore, I can stretch forth mine hands and hold all the creations which I have made; and mine eye can pierce them also, and among all the workmanship of mine hands there has not been so great wickedness as among thy brethren" (Moses 7:36).

We may now begin to appreciate why Jesus immediately began to feel very heavy and exceedingly sorrowful unto death. It was no less than the fall of Adam on this earth combined with all the effects of the Fall (including general sorrow, suffering, sickness, tribulation, and sin), combined with the individual sorrows and sins of every inhabitant of our earth, combined with all the sorrows and sins of the inhabitants of all the millions of earths like this one, combined with the fallen condition of every creature on this and all the other worlds, that caused the Savior to be pressed down by a weight such as no other being will ever experience.

Our finite mortal minds cannot grasp the tremendous load borne by the Savior in Gethsemane. But we begin to comprehend what this means in practical terms by remembering that this earth alone has had some 60 to 70 billion people live upon it during its temporal history. Each one of these 60 to 70 billion people has committed sin: "All have sinned and come short of the glory of God," Paul said (Romans 3:23). Multiply the sins, sorrows, heartaches, and injustices of these 60 to 70 billion souls by the millions of earths that the Savior created and redeemed, and we may begin to view the term "infinite atonement" in a different light. Gethsemane paid for all these things plus an infinitely possible combination of these things—even before they happened to us who live in modern times. Such is " the awful arithmetic of the Atonement," as Elder Neal A. Maxwell once said (*Ensign*, May 1985, 73). But even that is not all.

## SORE AMAZED

The Gospel of Mark is clear that Jesus felt something else in Gethsemane besides heaviness and sorrow. The King James Version translates the Greek *ekthambeisthai* as "sore amazed" (Mark 14:33). It is often rendered as "awestruck" or "astonished." One respected New Testament scholar says that this word is best rendered as "terrified surprise" (Murphy-O'Connor, "What Really Happened at Gethsemane," 36). What could possibly cause the Creator and Savior of worlds without number to feel surprised? It is difficult to conceive of something that the Savior did not know and hence would have been surprised over.

Yet, for all the things the Savior knew, there was one thing he did not know, and, in fact, could not know because of what he was. The scriptures declare with absolute certainty that Jesus was perfect, without sin. Paul testified, "For we have not an high priest which cannot be touched with the feeling of our infirmities; but was in all points tempted like as we are, yet without sin" (Hebrews 4:15).

Being perfect, Jesus did not and could not know what sin felt like. He did not have the experience of feeling the effects of sin—neither physically, spiritually, mentally, nor emotionally. Not until Gethsemane, that is. Now, in an instant, he began to feel all the sensations and effects of sin, all the guilt, anguish, darkness, turmoil, depression, anger, and physical sickness that sin brings. All of this the Savior felt and much, much more.

The shock to the Savior at this moment in his existence must have been overwhelming. Because he was perfect, he was also perfectly sensitive to all the effects and ramifications of sin on our mental, emotional, and physical makeup. His makeup was such that it could not tolerate sin or its effects, just as our systems cannot tolerate poison, disease, extreme heat, cold, dehydration, or a hundred other harmful substances and conditions. More significantly, as Mark describes for us, the experience Jesus had of finally comprehending sin as well as the feelings that issue from sin were absolutely surprising to him. He had never before experienced these sensations. Not only did it surprise him but it terrified him. For the first time in his eternal existence, the God of heaven and earth was experiencing the terrifying feelings associated with sin. Imagine! Jesus, the Eternal God of Old Testament times learned something in Gethsemane he had never known before. Perhaps that is the full meaning of Alma's words that the Son of God, the Messiah, would be born as a mortal so that "he may know *according to the flesh* how to succor his people" (Alma 7:12; emphasis added). Elder Maxwell summarizes this point: "Imagine, Jehovah, the Creator of this and other worlds, 'astonished'! Jesus knew cognitively what He must do, but not experientially. He had never personally known the exquisite and exacting process of an atonement before. Thus, when the agony came in its fulness, it was so much, much worse than even He with his unique intellect had ever imagined!" (*Ensign*, May 1985, 72–73).

Jesus Christ was a perfect God, a sinless God, but now he was also one who knew what sin felt like—even though he himself had committed no sin and even though his substitutionary experience with sin was terrifyingly surprising to him. Remember, he had before chided his apostles because they had been terrified and exhibited a lack of faith (Mark 4:40). Now, he himself knew terror. But in so discovering these new feelings, he became perfectly equipped to support and comfort each one of us in our moments of terrified surprise.

# HE CRIED, "ABBA"

Under the crushing weight of sin, sorrow, and suffering—all of which were originally ours but now had become his—and in a state of shock and terrified surprise, the Savior cried out in distress to his Father, just as a child might cry out for the comfort offered by a loving parent. The only relief the Savior could hope for might be found in prayer "that, if it were possible, the hour might pass from him" (Mark 14:35). Thus, in the most anguished cry of his life, the Savior pleaded, "Abba . . . all things are possible unto thee; take away this cup from me" (Mark 14:36).

To miss the significance of the word *Abba* at this point in the story of Gethsemane is to miss the true relationship that existed between Jesus and his Father. The word *Abba* is an Aramaic word meaning "Papa" or "Daddy." It is a form of address signifying the close, intimate, loving, and special bond that develops between some fathers and their children. The Gospel of Mark preserves a number of Aramaic words, it being the language of common discourse in Jesus' day, even among the learned rabbis.

I remember the first time I heard the word used in actual conversation. One of my Jewish studies professors in graduate school had invited some of us to attend synagogue services with his family. He had reserved a small classroom off to the side of the synagogue assembly hall to answer our questions after the service was over. His young daughter, four or five years old, was in the room with us. It was obvious that she was the apple of her father's eye, for when she kept interrupting his explanations, always beginning with "Abba," he would stop talking and rivet his attention on her—and always with a smile. Afterward, I asked him what *Abba* meant (although I was sure I knew). He answered with pride, "Why, *Daddy*, of course."

In Gethsemane, on that terrible but glorious night, in a scene so personal as almost to dissuade us from listening in, Jesus cried out in shockingly familiar tones, "Daddy (Papa), all things are possible for you. Please take this experience away—it is worse than even I thought it would be. Nevertheless, I will do what you desire and not what I desire."

It is important to remember that this plea was not theatrics. This petition really happened between a son and his father. It is a privileged communication, but we have been extended the privilege of learning about it because of God's love for us and his trust that we will hold it in reverence.

## TAKE AWAY THIS CUP

That Jesus reached the point where he wished not to partake of the bitter cup and asked his Father in intensely intimate, forthright terms to remove it, is evidenced in at least three ways.

First, Jesus' speech is reported essentially the same way in all three Synoptic Gospels: "take away," "remove," "let this pass." The Greek word translated as "cup" (*potērion*) also means "a person's lot" (as in lot in life) or even "dispensation." Three of the four Gospels unequivocally tell us that, frankly, things got so bad that Jesus was asking for any alternative to his unalterable course of suffering, any less horrible way to accomplish his Father's plan and purposes.

Second, the prophet Abinadi taught that in the atoning process the Savior subjugated his personal desires to his Father's desires, "the will of the Son being swallowed up in the will of the Father" (Mosiah 15:7). In this supreme act of meekness, he again set the example for us, showing us that subjecting our wills to the will of the Father is the monumental test of mortality. The Greek term for "will" used in Mark 14:36 ("nevertheless not what *I will*, but what thou *wilt*") is *thelo*, which means "to be willing, to desire, to prefer." Abinadi teaches us the true doctrine that Jesus' personal desires or preferences were brought into submission to the Father's desires. This is what Isaiah means when he says, "It pleased [the Father] to bruise him" (Isaiah 53:10). One gospel teacher put it this way:

> Begotten of an immortal Father and a mortal mother, Jesus possessed *two natures* (one divine, one human) and, therefore, *two wills* (that of the Father, and that of the Son). He could manifest either nature "at will." . . . The atonement required the subjection and sacrifice of the fleshly will of the "Son" to the spiritual will of the "Father." . . . The *Son* willed to let the cup pass; the *Father* willed that it should be drunk to its dregs. Abinadi described Jesus' submission as "the will of the Son being swallowed up in the will of the Father." . . . In a sense, it was not the Son *as* Son, but the Father *in* the Son who atoned. That is, Jesus not only did the will of his Father *in heaven*, but the will of the Father *in himself*. (Jackson, *1 Nephi to Alma 29*, 245)

Third, in his personal testimony about Gethsemane to the Prophet Joseph Smith, the Savior said that he "would [rather] . . . not drink the bitter cup" (D&C 19:18). Nevertheless, he did partake, and he finished his work on behalf of all humanity.

Rather than diminishing the Savior's accomplishment in Gethsemane by mentioning his personal preference to avoid suffering, we actually magnify it. When we acknowledge that

Jesus' submission to the Father's will was made in the face of having thought about other ways of accomplishing the Father's plan, we also acknowledge that he experienced every human emotion, every human thought, indeed, he descended below every human thought and every human desire. He demonstrated the human impulse to look for ways out of the horrors and agonies that constituted Gethsemane. The Savior's human nature wrestled with his divine nature. Yet, he was perfectly obedient. Most impressively, his obedience was informed obedience, not blind submission. There is no greater attribute than complete commitment with complete knowledge.

Will there not come a time—or many times—in our life when we will wrestle with conflicting impulses? Will there not come a time when each one of us will consciously have to choose to be obedient, to subjugate our desires and preferences to the will of God, to yield our agency to Deity? Our agency, our personal decision-making power, is really the only thing that is truly our private possession and domain—the only thing we "own" in mortality. To yield this ultimately personal possession to God is the greatest act of Christlike behavior we can engage in. Elder Neal A. Maxwell has said:

> The submission of one's will is really the only uniquely personal thing we have to place on God's altar. The many other things we "give," brothers and sisters, are actually the things He has already given or loaned to us. However, when you and I finally submit ourselves, by letting our individual wills be swallowed up in God's will, then we are really giving something to Him! It is the only possession which is truly ours to give!

Consecration thus constitutes the only unconditional surrender which is also a total victory! (*Ensign*, November 1995, 24)

In Gethsemane Jesus also demonstrated perfect meekness, for in the end he took what was thrust upon him without blaming other people or circumstances. Meekness may be thought of as poise under pressure, patience in the face of provocation. In another of his sermons, Elder Maxwell has provided us an example of the kind of meekness Jesus possessed in all its perfection:

> We even tend to think of a meek individual as being used and abused—as being a doormat for others. However, Moses was once described as being the most meek man on the face of the earth (see Num. 12:3), yet we recall his impressive boldness in the courts of Pharaoh and his scalding indignation following his descent from Sinai.
>
> President Brigham Young, who was tested in many ways and on many occasions, was once tried in a way that required him to "take it"—even from one he so much adored and admired. Brigham "took it" because he was meek. Yet, surely, none of us sitting here would think of Brigham Young as lacking in boldness or firmness! However, even President Young, in the closing and prestigious days of his life, spent some time in courtrooms being unjustifiably abused. When he might have chosen to assert himself politically, he "took it"—meekly. (*Ensign*, March 1983, 71)

We are told that each of us must cultivate the godly attribute of meekness. Meekness is not weakness. Rather, it is one of the clearest reflections of how closely our personality or makeup emulates the Savior's.

Thus, we return to two statements made by Paul in the book of Hebrews and marvel at the full, complete, and absolute truth the apostle teaches. Jesus confronted the full range of experiences, challenges, and decisions which all mortals face in this life. Yet, he remained our perfect exemplar and, thus, our perfect nurturer:

> Wherefore in all things it behoved him to be made like unto his brethren, that he might be a merciful and faithful high priest in things pertaining to God, to make reconciliation for the sins of the people.
>
> For in that he himself hath suffered being tempted, he is able to succour them that are tempted. (Hebrews 2:17–18)
>
> For we have not an high priest which cannot be touched with the feeling of our infirmities; but was in all points tempted like as we are, yet without sin.
>
> Let us therefore come boldly unto the throne of grace, that we may obtain mercy, and find grace to help in time of need. (Hebrews 4:15–16)

When it comes to describing the human condition, or our experience as frail mortals, nothing more profound has ever been spoken than the words, "Jesus knows what it's like!" He experienced it all for our sakes. The infinite and eternal God, who created the heavens and the earth, chose to come down to the earth to help us get back to heaven. He chose to become man so that we could become like God. He is able to show us the way to God because he knows the way of humans.

*And he came out, and went, as he was wont, to the mount of Olives; and his disciples also followed him.*

*And when he was at the place, he said unto them, Pray that ye enter not into temptation.*

*And he was withdrawn from them about a stone's cast, and kneeled down, and prayed,*

*Saying, Father, if thou be willing, remove this cup from me: nevertheless not my will, but thine, be done.*

*And there appeared an angel unto him from heaven, strengthening him.*

*And being in an agony he prayed more earnestly: and his sweat was as it were great drops of blood falling down to the ground.*

LUKE 22:39–44

# CHAPTER 4

# The Agony of the Bitter Cup

T he Gospel writer Luke gives us a unique perspective on Gethsemane. Luke was apparently not a member of the Quorum of the Twelve Apostles nor an eyewitness to the events of our Savior's life and ministry. He was a convert who received the apostolic witness with faith and magnified that witness in his own writings and in his missionary service. A lifelong companion to the apostle Paul (2 Timothy 4:11), Luke undoubtedly knew the other apostles and thus spoke of testimonies handed down to him by those who were "eye-witnesses, and ministers of the word" from the beginning (Luke 1:2).

Luke followed up his Gospel with a remarkable sequel, the Acts of the Apostles, which details in a powerful fashion the work of the Church leaders after the Savior's resurrection and ascension. But perhaps the real jewel in Luke's magnificent treasure trove of writings is Luke 22, particularly his description of the Savior's agony in Gethsemane. This is not because of any sensationalistic quality (I think we actually recoil from such graphic descriptions of God's sufferings) but rather because of its unique details and singular lesson on what the Atonement cost—what price was paid. In fact, reading Luke 22 prompts us to cry out, "If a being who is all-powerful suffers that much, what hope is there for any of us? It looks like no one is immune from suffering!"

That is precisely the point. No one *is* immune from the trials, tribulations, and sufferings of mortality. But because Jesus did suffer so much, we don't have to.

## An Angel from Heaven—Mighty Michael

In describing Jesus' experience in Gethsemane, Luke confirms many details found in the other three Gospels. Jesus left the upper room and went "as he was wont, to the mount of Olives" (Luke 22:39). Jesus was accustomed to going to Gethsemane, as John indicates (John 18:1–2). There Jesus instructed the apostles on guarding against temptation (Matthew 26:41) and then moved into the garden a stone's throw farther distant, at which point he began to petition the Father to remove the bitter cup (Mark 13:35).

But his pleadings were tempered by his stated commitment to obey the Father's will. Undoubtedly, the author of Hebrews 5:8–9 had in mind this very moment in Gethsemane when he wrote: "Though he were a Son [meaning God's literal Son who occupied a special position], yet learned he obedience by [or because of] the things which he suffered. . . . and . . . he became the author of eternal salvation unto all them that obey him."

This passage portrays the doctrinal essence of Gethsemane. Just as Jesus became the author of eternal salvation by obeying the Father, all of us must obey Jesus if we want to partake of that salvation and become like the Father.

Luke's narrative also includes a stunning detail not found

anywhere else in the New Testament. An angel appeared to the Savior for the express purpose of strengthening him in his extremity.

Who cannot be moved by this scene? Under extreme duress, Jesus pleads with his Father to remove the bitter cup. This Son is the Well Beloved Son. He has never done anything wrong, never! He is perfect and has always sought to honor his Father, to do everything right and good and compassionate.

But the one thing the Father cannot now do for his perfect Son is the very thing his Well Beloved Son has suggested— remove the bitter cup. He must watch his Son go through all this agony and more. Perhaps it is no exaggeration to say that at that fateful moment in the Garden of Gethsemane almost two thousand years ago, two divine Beings suffered and sacrificed to bring about an eternity's worth of possibilities for you and me and billions upon billions of others.

Latter-day Saint author Edwin W. Aldous has said: "The Father himself witnessed the intense physical and spiritual agony of his Only Begotten Son in Gethsemane and on the cross. And, just as he can remove our pain, he could have spared his Son that agony; indeed, he had the power to remove the bitter cup from the Savior, but the consequences were unacceptable" ("Reflection on the Atonement's Healing Power," 13). Brother Aldous also mentions a well-known statement by Elder Melvin J. Ballard of the Quorum of the Twelve Apostles, which is one of the grandest insights into this moment in Gethsemane that has ever been written:

> In that moment when he might have saved his Son, I thank him and praise him that he did not fail us, for he had not only the love of his Son in mind, but he also

had love for us. I rejoice that he did not interfere, and that his love for us made it possible for him to endure to look upon the sufferings of his Son and give him finally to us, our Savior and our Redeemer. Without him, without his sacrifice, we would have remained, and we would never have come glorified in his presence. And so this is what it cost, in part, for our Father in Heaven to give the gift of his Son unto men. (Hinckley, *Sermons and Missionary Services of Melvin Joseph Ballard*, 154–55)

If the scene in Gethsemane plays on our emotions, if it tugs at our heartstrings, that is well and good. It ought to, for it is at the very heart of who we are and what we can become.

Another apostle, Elder Jeffrey R. Holland, in a more recent day also spoke to the issue of our Heavenly Father not removing the bitter cup from his Only Begotten Son. In an Easter general conference address on 3 April 1999, Elder Holland began:

I wish to thank not only the resurrected Lord Jesus Christ but also His true Father, our spiritual Father and God, who, by accepting the sacrifice of His firstborn, perfect Son, blessed all of His children in those hours of atonement and redemption. Never more than at Easter time is there so much meaning in that declaration from the book of John which praises the Father as well as the Son: "For God so loved the world, that he gave his only begotten Son, that whosoever believeth in him should not perish, but have everlasting life." (John 3:16)

I am a father, inadequate to be sure, but I cannot comprehend the burden it must have been for God in His heaven to witness the deep suffering and Crucifixion of His Beloved Son in such a manner. His every impulse and instinct must have been to stop it, to send angels to intervene—but He did not intervene. He endured what He saw because it was the only way that a saving, vicarious payment could be made for the sins of all His other children, from Adam and Eve to the end of the world. I am eternally grateful for a perfect Father and His perfect Son, neither of whom shrank from the bitter cup nor forsook the rest of us who are imperfect, who fall short and stumble, who too often miss the mark. (*Ensign*, May 1999, 14)

Our Heavenly Father could not, would not, take away the bitter cup. Thankfully, he did not shrink from the bitter cup, just as his Son did not shrink from it. But our Heavenly Father did send needed help in the form of an angel to minister to his Son.

Undoubtedly, many have wondered about the identity of that angel sent from the heavenly courts. Elder Bruce R. McConkie believed it to have been Michael, or Adam, the Ancient of Days and the father of the human family on this earth (*Ensign*, May 1985, 9).

Why Michael? Why would our Heavenly Father choose him, or why would he have been allowed to perform so noble a task? Choosing Michael makes perfect sense. Besides the sins of all humankind, for whose single, separate, and unique transgression was Jesus paying the debt owed to justice?

The apostle Paul taught, "For since by man came death, by man came also the resurrection of the dead. For as in Adam all die, even so in Christ shall all be made alive" (1 Corinthians 15:21–22). That is to say, the Savior's atoning work in

71

Gethsemane is directly linked to Adam's transgression, which brought about the fall of man. The Creation, the Fall, and the Atonement are inextricably linked as the three pillars of eternity, the three central events upon which the Father's plan rests. Who better than Adam to aid and assist the Savior during his time of extreme distress than he whose actions had brought about mortality? Who better to thank the Savior for paying the debt that his actions had introduced (sin, suffering, and the other myriad effects of the Fall) than Adam himself? Who better to strengthen the Great Creator than he who, as one of the gods, assisted the Savior in laying the foundations of the very planet where the Savior himself, as well as all the children of Adam, would someday reside? Who better to minister to the mortal Jesus than one of his own mortal ancestors, for Adam was in very deed a forefather of the Savior's mother, Mary.

## JESUS LEFT ALONE

All of these reasons and others help us to understand why the Father could have sent mighty Michael to stand in his own stead and minister to his Only Begotten Son. He could not remove the bitter cup from his Son because that was the very reason his Son had been sent into the world—to redeem the entire family of God (John 18:37). Nor could the Father himself come to the aid of his Son, for that would not have given the Son the complete victory he needed to have over sin, sorrow, suffering, hell, and the effects of the Fall. The Father is pure, glorified, unadulterated life, and in Gethsemane the Savior had to experience *all* things, even descend *below* all things, to satisfy the demands of justice. The things he had to experience included spiritual death, the withdrawal of the Father and the removal of his immediate influence (which

72

experience later returned to the Savior as he hung on the cross)—in truth, the atmosphere of hell itself.

In Gethsemane, Jesus was left alone by the Father. He was engulfed in darkness, spiritual death, and the agony of hell. He descended below the level of anything ever experienced by any man or woman. All mortals possess a measure (to a greater or lesser degree) of the Lord's Spirit. But Jesus possessed the Spirit in its fulness (John 3:34; JST John 3:34). The shock of the Spirit's withdrawal, the withdrawal of light and life, was overwhelmingly traumatic and plunged Jesus into hell. His victory over all things demanded it.

The Book of Mormon prophet Jacob taught that "spiritual death is hell" (2 Nephi 9:12). The Prophet Joseph Smith learned that spiritual death comes when man is separated from God's presence and influence (D&C 29:40–41). "For Jesus to take upon Himself the consequences of sin required that he suffer spiritual death for all men" (Andrus, *God, Man, and the Universe*, 424).

Thus, our Father in Heaven left his Beloved Son alone to suffer the pains of hell, and out of that wrenching crucible, Jesus gained the victory. Elder James E. Talmage said:

> From the terrible conflict in Gethsemane, Christ emerged a victor. Though in the dark tribulation of that fearful hour He had pleaded that the bitter cup be removed from His lips, the request, however oft repeated, was always conditional; the accomplishment of the Father's will was never lost sight of as the object of the Son's supreme desire. The further tragedy of the night, and the cruel inflictions that awaited Him on the morrow, to culminate in the frightful tortures of the

cross, could not exceed the bitter anguish through which He had successfully passed. (*Jesus the Christ*, 614)

The Father could not assist his Son directly, but he sent an angel to strengthen him. The human family was saved by one of its own, and the Saving One was strengthened by one of his own—his many times over great-grandfather Adam.

## HE PRAYED MORE EARNESTLY

From Luke's inspired description, we begin to comprehend that the Savior's anguish and suffering was unrelenting. In fact, it increased and increased—more pressure, more torture, more agony. "And being in an agony he prayed more earnestly" (Luke 22:44). Here the Savior of the universe teaches us through his experience that all prayers are not alike, nor are they expected to be. A greater need, a more intense life circumstance, calls forth from us more earnest, faith-filled petition and pleading.

I remember hearing as a young deacon a priesthood lesson on prayer given by a man that I and the other members of my quorum were very fond of. He talked about the need for profound respect when approaching God in prayer and spoke of several other important matters relative to prayer, including the how's and why's. And then he said, "But I'll tell you a little secret. It's when you are in the middle of a crisis that you really learn about prayer."

He told us about a time when his infant son became sick and then died, how his prayers were different because he and his wife pleaded with such intensity, and about how it felt to really talk with our Father in Heaven. His counsel had a great effect. It is not the words we speak or the language we use that is important. What really matters is getting down to admitting with all our hearts that we need God's help.

Since those days of my youth, I have come to appreciate what our deacons' quorum leader meant and how such experiences help us understand the lessons in Luke's description of the Savior's more earnest pleadings. Not all prayers are alike. As with the Savior, so with us. Some prayers will be more earnest than others.

President Joseph F. Smith also taught that it is intensity of spirit much more than eloquence of language that constitutes sincere prayer:

> It is not such a difficult thing to learn how to pray. It is not the words we use particularly that constitute prayer. . . . True, faithful, earnest prayer consists more in the feeling that rises from the heart and from the inward desire of our spirits to supplicate the Lord in humility and in faith, that we may receive his blessings. It matters not how simple the words may be, if our desires are genuine and we come before the Lord with a broken heart and contrite spirit to ask him for that which we need. (*Gospel Doctrine*, 219)

President Smith's counsel links our prayers with those of the Savior's experience in Gethsemane. A "broken heart and contrite spirit" were displayed by the Savior as he worked out the infinite and eternal atonement. We must acquire the same characteristics.

President Harold B. Lee taught something about prayer that strikes a responsive chord as we seek to comprehend the Savior's experience in Gethsemane: "The most important thing you can do is to learn to talk to God. Talk to Him as you would talk to your father, for He is your Father, and He wants you to talk to Him" (*Church News*, 3 March 1973, 3).

The scriptures are full of examples of people who, like the Savior, talked with God as their Father in an intimate way and found that a greater need calls forth a more earnest, intense, and yearning prayer. Moses, Hannah, Solomon, Hezekiah, Lehi, Nephi, Enos, and Zechariah, the father of John the Baptist, are just a few examples.

## GREAT DROPS OF BLOOD

So intense did Jesus' agony in Gethsemane become that he began to sweat great drops of blood. Some scholars have suggested that the Savior's sweating blood was not an actual occurrence (because some of these verses do not appear in the earliest manuscripts of Luke's Gospel) or that a later editor of Luke's record intended to convey that his sweat was so profuse that it fell to the ground in the same way drops of blood fall to the ground, or even that this portion of Luke's story is entirely allegorical. Latter-day Saints, however, have been spared any doubt about the essential truth of Luke's description because the Savior himself has given us his own testimony of the reality of his exquisite agony (Mosiah 3:7; D&C 19:16–19). Likewise, the Joseph Smith Translation of these verses in Luke testify of their validity. Truly, Jesus bled from every pore in Gethsemane.

Such a condition as Jesus experienced is not unknown. A remarkable article in the *Journal of the American Medical Association* discusses the rare phenomenon called hematidrosis (bloody sweat) as the very real condition described by Luke. It has been known to occur in persons with bleeding disorders, or, more significantly, in persons experiencing extreme distress and highly emotional states. As a result of extreme stress and pressure, the small blood vessels just under the skin hemorrhage. Blood mixes with perspiration, and the skin becomes fragile and tender. Thus, in the cold night air, this condition may have also produced chills in Jesus. Some have further suggested that the hematidrosis suffered by Jesus also produced hypovolemia, or shock due to excessive loss of bodily fluid (Edwards, Gabel, and Hosmer, "On the Physical Death of Jesus," 1455–56).

That Luke alone in the New Testament preserves the scene of the Savior's bloody trauma in Gethsemane becomes all the more noteworthy when we realize that he was a physician (Colossians 4:14). It is only natural that he be interested in the physical effects of Gethsemane on the Savior's body. Luke, in fact, preserves a number of observations about trauma, healing, and the physical body in his writings, precisely because he was a physician and well trained in observing disorders of the human body. With respect to Jesus, Luke would have us know without equivocation that "no other man, however great his powers of physical or mental endurance, could have suffered so; for his human organism would have succumbed, and syncope would have produced unconsciousness and welcome oblivion" (Talmage, *Jesus the Christ*, 613).

## JESUS AND THE OLIVE

That Jesus bled from every pore in Gethsemane is significant in two ways. First, the literal significance is that he shed his blood for us twice: in the garden and on the cross. His atoning blood in Gethsemane was no less important than his atoning blood on the cross. Thus, Jesus approached death twice: in the garden and on the cross—which is where he finally yielded up his life. But Gethsemane was also slow agony—death by degrees—and the results of Jesus' trauma in Gethsemane came back to torment him during his trial. When he was stripped of his clothing before he was crucified (Matthew 27:26–28), the dried blood from his pores would have been pulled away from the tender flesh and inflicted even more pain.

Second, the symbolic significance of Jesus shedding his blood in Gethsemane has to do with the very place where it all happened. Gethsemane, the garden of the "oil press" on the Mount of Olives, is where olives were crushed to harvest their oil. Under extreme weight and pressure, the olives yielded their valuable fluid. Under extreme weight and pressure, Jesus bled from every pore. In Gethsemane, not only did Jesus become us but he became the olive. In the garden of the oil press, where olives were pressed out, Jesus himself was pressed out.

This symbolic correspondence is no accident, and there are many parallels between Jesus and the olive and between the Atonement and the pressing process that are not mere coincidences. In ancient Israel, the olive tree was supreme among all others, as reflected in scripture. First mentioned in connection with the Great Flood, the dove released by Noah returned to the ark with an olive leaf in her mouth, signifying that the waters were abating (Genesis 8:11). Thus, by the appearance together of these two symbolic objects, the dove and olive leaf, the promise of continuing life on earth and peace with Deity was assured. Later in the Pentateuch, olive trees are mentioned in the early descriptions of Canaan, signifying both that the land was a holy land of promise given by Deity to Israel and that the olive tree itself was a gift from God:

> And it shall be, when the Lord thy God shall have brought thee into the land which he sware unto thy

fathers, to Abraham, to Isaac, and to Jacob, to give thee great and goodly cities, which thou buildedst not,

And houses full of all good things, which thou filledst not, and wells digged, which thou diggedst not, vineyards and olive trees, which thou plantedst not; when thou shalt have eaten and be full. (Deuteronomy 6:10–11)

Jeremiah 11:16 indicates that even Israel itself was called by Jehovah "a green olive tree, fair, and of goodly fruit." Later rabbinic commentary expounded on that symbolism: "Israel was called 'an olive tree, leafy and fair' because they [Israel] shed light on all" (*Shmot Raba* 36.1). This imagery undoubtedly came from the coloration of the olive leaf itself as well as the fact that the oil was burned for light.

It is not simple happenstance that when Gideon's youngest son, Jotham, climbed Mount Gerizim and proclaimed a parable to the citizens of Shechem, the olive tree was given pride of place:

And when they told it to Jotham, he went and stood in the top of mount Gerizim, and lifted up his voice, and cried, and said unto them, Hearken unto me, ye men of Shechem, that God may hearken unto you.

The trees went forth on a time to anoint a king over them; and they said unto the olive tree, Reign thou over us.

But the olive tree said unto them, Should I leave my fatness, wherewith by me they honor God and man, and go to be promoted over the trees?

And the trees said to the fig tree, Come thou, and reign over us.

But the fig tree said unto them, Should I forsake my

sweetness, and my good fruit, and go to be promoted over the trees? (Judges 9:7–11)

One reason the olive tree was foremost among all others was that it was used to worship God as well as to sustain the life of mankind. The olive tree and its oil were unequivocally regarded as a necessity of life. In fact, nothing from the olive tree went unused in the daily life of Israel. The oil from the fruit—the olives—was used for cooking, lighting, medicine, lubrication, and anointing. Olives not crushed and pressed were pickled in brine and spices and then eaten. The wood of the olive tree was used in constructing buildings and carved into furniture, ornaments, and tools, including the shepherd's crook, or staff. We may truly say that the olive tree was (and continues to be) a staff of life in the Middle East.

Olive trees were even more abundant in the Holy Land in Jesus' day than they are today. In fact, the olive tree was anciently both a religious and a national symbol for the people of Israel, and its fruit was an important domestic and exported product in the biblical period. In Old Testament times, virtually every village and even most houses had a small oil press to supply families with the necessities of life deriving from olive cultivation. By New Testament times, olive crushers made of stone and lever presses were quite plentiful throughout the land.

Techniques of olive production in modern times suggest the way olives were cultivated, harvested, and processed in ancient times. Olive trees do not mature quickly, and the best yields come only after twelve or more years of patient care—a circumstance that requires a certain degree of settlement and peace. But with only a little attention, an adult olive tree will continue to produce heavily, usually every other year, for hundreds of years. Yield from a good tree was expected to run anywhere from ten to fifteen gallons each season.

Production of olive oil anciently was a time-consuming undertaking. It consisted of six basic steps or procedures:

1. *Harvesting* the olives. Some, of course, were left for the poor, the fatherless, the widow, or the sojourner, as scripture required (Deuteronomy 24:19–21; Leviticus 19:9–10; Ruth 2:2–3). Olives in ancient times were harvested during the period from September to late October, right after the first rains, which signaled the time for the harvest to begin. Growers in the Holy Land today still follow this timetable.

2. *Separating* the olives into two groups. Olives for pickling were separated from those to be crushed for oil.

3. *Crushing* the olives intended for oil. Crushing the olives— pits and all—produced a pasty, oily mash, or pulp. In Old Testament times, the crushing was done with a millstone or by pounding from human feet in a rock-hewn press, even a winepress (Deuteronomy 33:24; Micah 6:15). By New Testament times, olives were crushed in a specially carved rock basin called a *yam*. A crushing wheel made of stone was fitted snugly inside the stone basin and either pushed around the interior of the basin by a strong man or pulled around it by a beast of burden.

4. *Gathering* the crushed pulp from the *yam*. The pulp was collected and placed in flat, round, woven baskets. The baskets, usually about two feet in diameter and three to four inches high, were stacked two or three high under one of two traditional kinds of presses—a lever press or a screw press. The

lever press consisted of a long heavy wooden beam with huge stone weights attached to the end of the beam opposite the woven baskets. Use of the lever press can be dated to the early Iron Age, around the tenth century before Christ. The screw press was not used until the late Hellenistic period, beginning about the first century before Christ. It consisted of a giant wooden screw carved from a large piece of olive wood with a handle attached to its top so it could be turned. The screw was held in place by a large frame. Turning the screw applied increasing pressure to the baskets containing the olive mash.

5. *Pressing* the olive pulp. Pressure applied to the olive mash in the baskets stacked under the press caused oil to ooze out of the baskets and run down a shallow channel into a collection pit. Hot water could be poured over the baskets being squeezed to increase the flow of oil. Unlike modern processes involving hydraulic presses, the pressing procedure in ancient times took many hours, even days, with pressure constantly being increased.

6. *Refining* the oil by allowing it to sit for several days in the collection pit. When the oil flowed into the collection basin, it consisted of two liquids: the pure olive oil and a heavier, watery, sediment-filled liquid called the dregs. When the two liquids were allowed to set up, or settle, the pure oil rose to the top and was either skimmed off by hand or allowed to spill over into another collecting vat, where the settling process was repeated to further refine the oil.

This cultural and historical background helps us to more fully understand the profoundly symbolic relationship between the olive, the Savior, and the Atonement. We appreciate the symbolic significance of Jesus' experience in Gethsemane all the more when we remember that—

1. Just as olives are one of seven native fruits indigenous to the Holy Land (Deuteronomy 8:8), so was Jesus a native of the Holy Land. Moreover, the ancient rabbis likened Judah, the lineage of Jesus, to the olive tree (Babylonian Talmud, Menahoth, 53b).

2. Just as at least one strand of Jewish tradition identifies the tree of life as the olive tree, so does the Book of Mormon equate Jesus Christ with the tree of life and identify his atonement as the reality behind the symbol of the *fruit* of the tree of life in Lehi's dream (Ginzberg, *Legends of the Jews*, 1:93; 2:119; 1 Nephi 11:21–22, 25–33).

3. Just as in Jewish tradition the olive tree is called the tree of light (*Shmot Raba* 36.1) and a symbol of "light to the world" (*Tankhuma Tzave* 5.1), so too is Jesus the "Light of the World" (John 1:4–5; 8:12; 9:5; D&C 11:28). Anciently, the Temple *menorah* ("candlestick") was lit with "'pure oil of pounded olives'—not with walnut oil or radish [seed] oil, but only with olive oil which is a light unto the world.' However, it is not only the olive oil which gives forth light, but also the olive tree itself" (Hareuveni, *Nature in Our Biblical Heritage*, 134). In addition, in ancient times only pure olive oil could be used for the Sabbath lamps (Mishnah, *Shabbat* 26a).

4. Just as the olive branch has been regarded as a universal symbol of peace from earliest times, so too is Jesus the Prince of Peace whose recognition will someday be universal (Romans

14:11). This is the message of Doctrine and Covenants 88, which "was designated by the Prophet as the 'olive leaf . . . plucked from the Tree of Paradise, the Lord's message of peace to us'" (headnote to D&C 88).

5.   Just as olives are best picked individually so as not to damage the tree (ideally, the olives are not stripped from the branches), so too is Christ's love individual. If alternative methods of harvesting the olives, such as stripping the branches or beating the tree (Deuteronomy 24:20) are used to finish the harvest more quickly, the tree may be damaged. As with olives, so too with souls; it takes time and effort on an individual basis to effectively harvest both. But even the process of "beating" the tree is itself symbolic of the atoning act of the Savior (Isaiah 53:4–5); perhaps that is why the scriptures permit this method of harvest.

6.   Just as the connection is literal between the meaning of the word *Gethsemane* ("oil press") and what was done there agriculturally, so is the connection profoundly symbolic between *Gethsemane* and what Jesus did there in the last hours of his mortal life.

7.   Just as the life fluid of the olives was pressed out by the intense pressure of the crushing stone rolling over them in the stone basin, so too was the goodness and perfection of Jesus' life "harvested" in Gethsemane. There he was "bruised," as Isaiah prophesied (Isaiah 53:5), and there his life fluid, his blood, was pressed out by the crushing weight of sin and the extreme pressure of spiritual agony.

8.   Just as the bitter taste of the olive pulp is removed in the pressing process (olives straight from the tree are exquisitely

bitter) and the remaining oil actually has a kind of sweet flavor, so too is the bitterness of mortal life, brought on by sin and the other effects of the fall of Adam, removed or "pressed out" by Christ's atonement (D&C 19:16–19). For example, nothing was so "sweet" to Alma as his joy over being redeemed through the atonement of Christ (Alma 36:21).

9. Just as the color of the oil from the best olives at first runs red in the crusher at the beginning of each pressing season, so too was the perspiration of the best, finest, purest Being on earth turned red as he bled from every pore (Luke 22:44). Pure, fresh olive oil is the perfect symbol of Christ's blood. Such imagery turns our thoughts not just to the Savior's first coming but also to his second coming, as taught in the scriptures:

> And it shall be said: Who is this that cometh down from God in heaven with dyed garments; yea, from the regions which are not known, clothed in his glorious apparel, traveling in the greatness of his strength?
>
> And he shall say: I am he who spake in righteousness, mighty to save.
>
> And the Lord shall be red in his apparel, and his garments like him that treadeth in the wine-vat. . . .
>
> And his voice shall be heard: I have trodden the wine-press alone, and have brought judgment upon all people; and none were with me. (D&C 133:46–50)

The connection in ancient times between oil presses and wine presses was a real one. Wine presses were sometimes used as oil presses to crush olives when they were trodden out with the feet (Micah 6:15), and thus the presses were regarded as interchangeable.

10. Just as the pressure on the olives under the press became more intense with each passing moment and the olives exuded more of their oil as more pressure was applied, so too did the pressure on the Savior in the garden become more intense over time and put him under greater stress the longer he was in Gethsemane, the place called the "oil press" (Luke 22:39–44; Matthew 26:36–45).

11. Just as pure olive oil was used as a healing agent for the physical body in the ancient world—a concept taught by the parable of the good Samaritan (Luke 10:34)—so too the Atonement, the product of the pressing process in Gethsemane, is the greatest healing agent in all the universe, "worlds without number" (Moses 1:33; D&C 76:42–43). Christ is truly the "balm in Gilead" (Jeremiah 8:22).

12. Just as the olive-pressing process yields the purest and brightest burning of vegetable oils—a fact known in ancient Israel (Exodus 27:20)—so too the pressing process in Gethsemane involved the purest and brightest burning, in terms of eternal glory, of the Father's children.

13. Just as the refined product of bruised, crushed, and pressed olives—the pure olive oil—is consecrated and set apart for healing of the sick, so too the purest of God's children was consecrated and set apart in premortality to be bruised, crushed, and pressed for our "sicknesses" and "pains" as well as our sins (Alma 7:11) so that we can be healed both physically and spiritually.

14. Just as pure olive oil was used in the temple in ancient times for anointing (Leviticus 8:6–12), so is it similarly used today in the Lord's temples, those buildings in which we learn the most about the Anointed One. Every aspect of temple worship centers on, is grounded in, and points us to the Savior and his atonement.

15. Just as in ancient times Israel anointed her prophets, priests, and kings with olive oil (Exodus 30:30; 2 Samuel 2:4; 1 Kings 19:16), so was Jesus anointed to become the Redeemer (D&C 138:42). In fact, the anointing of Israel's prophets, priests, and kings was done as a type and shadow of the Anointed One to come (Hebrew, *mashiach*; English, *Messiah*). The Anointed One is the true Prophet, Priest, and King of all eternity, as testified of in the hymn: "I know that my Redeemer lives. . . . He lives, my prophet, priest, and king" (*Hymns*, no. 136).

16. Just as Deuteronomy 21:23 foreshadowed the death of the Messiah upon a "tree," so history teaches that the Roman crosses used for crucifixions in Palestine were often solidly rooted olive trees with most of their branches removed and a crossbar attached. This image is presented by the apostle Paul in his epistle to the Galatians on the merits and mercies of Christ (Galatians 3:13). Ironically, he describes Jesus, who is symbolized by the olive tree, as being crucified on an olive tree.

17. Just as in ancient times the anointing with olive oil and even the horn in which the oil was kept were linked to the Messiah, so the anointing with olive oil and its container are linked to Jesus. In ancient times, olive oil was kept in a

horn, the well-recognized repository for the anointing agent (1 Samuel 16:13). The Hebrew idiom "horn of salvation" signified the Messiah's great power to judge and save (1 Samuel 2:10; 2 Samuel 22:3; Psalm 18:2; 132:17). Likewise is Jesus symbolized by the horn of oil, which represents his power. Zacharias said of Jesus, the Messiah, at the time his own son, John the Baptist, was born: "Blessed be the Lord God of Israel; for he hath visited and redeemed his people. And hath raised up an *horn* of salvation for us in the house of his servant David" (Luke 1:68–69).

18. Just as we cannot anoint and consecrate ourselves with olive oil to perform ordinances on ourselves (we can only anoint and consecrate others), so too only another, the Anointed One, could make an infinite and eternal atonement on our behalf (Alma 34:9–15). As we serve others by anointing them, we imitate the Messiah, who served not himself but us by consecrating his life.

19. Just as the prophets Zenos and Jacob (like Paul in his epistle to the Romans) depict the scattering and gathering of Israel through the imagery of the tame and the wild olive trees, so the Book of Mormon teaches that the scatterer and gatherer of Israel is Jesus Christ himself: "All the people who are of the house of Israel, will *I* gather in, saith the Lord, according to the words of the prophet Zenos" (1 Nephi 19:16; emphasis added). Israel is gathered first and foremost to Jesus Christ.

20. Just as putting oil in the lamp was a common, everyday necessity in the ancient world, so has "oil in the lamp"

become a powerful metaphor signifying faithfulness and readiness for the time of the Anointed One's second coming (Matthew 25:1–13). "Wherefore, be faithful, praying always, having your lamps trimmed and burning, and oil with you, that you may be ready at the coming of the Bridegroom" (D&C 33:17; 45:56–57).

Other symbolism of this kind can surely be enumerated, but there is one emblem to which my mind returns again and again. The pure olive oil that priesthood holders use to anoint the sick and that temple officiators, both men and women, use to anoint those being endowed is, without doubt, the supreme symbol of the Savior's blood and his atoning sacrifice offered in Gethsemane. We use this emblem, symbolic of the True Healing Agent, to demonstrate our faith in his ability to heal the sick in mortality as well as consecrate the pure in heart in our temples.

## GETHSEMANE AND A MODERN EXPERIENCE

As a student of the Savior's experience in Gethsemane, I had a profound experience which will forever remain etched in my memory. Brigham Young University maintains a study center on the Mount of Olives, overlooking the very places of our Lord's ministry. Three olive presses are situated on the grounds, where they serve both as object lessons and as invitations to explore ancient olive culture.

One fall semester I supervised the students at the BYU Jerusalem Center as they participated in their own olive harvest and pressing activity. The olives were placed in the *yam*, or rock basin, and the crushing stone was pushed around and around the basin until the olives began to ooze their oil. When the oil began to run down the lip of the limestone basin, it had the distinctive red color characteristic of the first moments of the new pressing each year.

At that instant an audible gasp came from the 170 students who surrounded the olive press to witness our re-creation of the ancient pressing process. It was a stunning, even chilling, minute until the oil turned back to its usual golden color. I believe everyone in that group had the same thought as we watched this happen. It was more than just an amazing confirmation of the symbolism we had discussed. This was, right before our very eyes, a real-life reflection of Gethsemane.

As those who have lived in or visited the Holy Land know, a person cannot escape the image of the olive tree. Olive vineyards and ancient olive presses seem to be everywhere, and visitors' hearts and minds become acutely attuned to their existence. Especially after witnessing an olive harvest, visitors never look at olive trees the same way again. They never regard them as they might have in the past, never view them as being common or an ordinary part of the landscape.

Olive trees are extraordinary trees in an extraordinary land. They are part of the landscape of belief. It is not by accident that we anoint those seeking a blessing with olive oil. Olive trees and the oil derived from their fruit are the most powerful and plentiful symbols in the Holy Land of Jesus Christ, the Master Healer, who was born into a land with abundant reminders of his divinity.

Olive trees are witnesses of his and his Father's love. Just as olive trees and olive oil are gifts from God (Deuteronomy 6:10–11; 11:14), so too is the Savior our great gift from God (John 3:16), and the effects which flow from his atonement—

eternal life—"is the greatest of all the gifts of God" (D&C 14:7). In the place called the "oil press," Gethsemane, the Savior was pressed in our behalf as he wrought for all mankind the infinite and eternal atonement. Just as the olive tree and olive oil may sustain our lives temporally, so does the Savior sustain our lives eternally.

And he went a little further, and fell on his face, and prayed, saying, O my Father, if it be possible, let this cup pass from me: nevertheless not as I will, but as thou wilt.

And he cometh unto the disciples, and findeth them asleep, and saith unto Peter, What, could ye not watch with me one hour?

Watch and pray, that ye enter not into temptation: the spirit indeed is willing, but the flesh is weak.

He went away again the second time, and prayed, saying O my Father, if this cup may not pass away from me, except I drink it, thy will be done.

And he came and found them asleep again: for their eyes were heavy.

And he left them, and went away again, and prayed the third time, saying the same words.

Then cometh he to his disciples, and saith unto them, Sleep on now, and take your rest: behold, the hour is at hand, and the Son of man is betrayed into the hands of sinners.

Rise, let us be going: behold, he is at hand that doth betray me.

MATTHEW 26:39–46

# CHAPTER 5

# The Intensity of the Bitter Cup

Matthew, who was also known as Levi (Matthew 9:9; Mark 2:14), was a member of the Quorum of the Twelve Apostles and a powerful witness of the Lord's atoning sacrifice. His Gospel, according to the early Church historian Eusebius (ca. A.D. 340), was written and preserved in Aramaic, the very language in which Jesus prayed in Gethsemane.

Matthew was a gifted writer who wanted the Jews to see that Jesus was the promised King-Messiah, the singular prophet of whom Moses had prophesied (Deuteronomy 18:18) and, thus, the new Moses, the very One whose life followed the pattern of the life of the Old Testament lawgiver and deliverer.

Matthew's testimony of the Savior's suffering in Gethsemane helps us more fully understand his experience in the garden and rounds out our picture of the intensity of his agony. We sense that Matthew tells the story with real feeling.

# HE PRAYED THE THIRD TIME

Unique to Matthew's report of Gethsemane is the observation that Jesus prayed three times, "saying the same words" (Matthew 26:44). This fact is confirmed in a remarkable vision beheld by Orson F. Whitney (1855–1931) several years before he was ordained an apostle. Brother Whitney regarded this singular event as the turning point in his life and traced all future success to this vision:

> I seemed to be in the Garden of Gethsemane, a witness of the Savior's agony. I saw Him as plainly as ever I have seen anyone. Standing behind a tree in the foreground, I beheld Jesus, with Peter, James and John, as they came through a little . . . gate at my right. Leaving the three Apostles there, after telling them to kneel and pray, the Son of God passed over to the other side, where He also knelt and prayed. It was the same prayer with which all Bible readers are familiar: "Oh my Father, if it be possible, let this cup pass from me; nevertheless not as I will, but as thou wilt."
>
> As He prayed the tears streamed down his face, which was toward me. I was so moved at the sight that I also wept, out of pure sympathy. My whole heart went out to him; I loved him with all my soul, and longed to be with him as I longed for nothing else.
>
> Presently He arose and walked to where those Apostles were kneeling—fast asleep! He shook them gently, awoke them, and in a tone of tender reproach, untinctured by the least show of anger or impatience, asked them plaintively if they could not watch with him one hour. There He was, with the awful weight of the

world's sin upon his shoulders, with the pangs of every man, woman and child shooting through his sensitive soul—and they could not watch with him one poor hour!

Returning to his place, He offered up the same prayer as before; then went back and again found them sleeping. Again he awoke them, readmonished them, and once more returned and prayed. Three times this occurred. (*Through Memory's Halls*, 82)

We can scarcely fail to be moved by so tender a description: the tears of the Savior himself, his anguish and feelings of being alone, the tears of Brother Whitney, and, above all, the impression of relentless agony.

This description, like Matthew's, paints the picture of a man coming apart; a man unraveling or breaking down physiologically and mentally; a man trying to find some respite from a true physical and spiritual ordeal; a man looking for any kind of relief after prayers, one after the other, that did not yield any relief; a man seeking relief from the weight of sin, sorrow, suffering—even if only for a moment—by getting up to check on trusted associates and to seek some support. No relief was to be found for those intense moments—how long they lasted we do not know. There would be no relief until justice had been satisfied, and that was only until all the agony returned as Jesus hung on the cross on Calvary's hill.

Elder Whitney's description brings to mind a phrase to depict Gethsemane: blood, sweat, and tears—all belonging to Jesus. The New Testament does not mention tears, but Elder Whitney is our confirming witness that tears of sorrow and suffering mingled with Jesus' blood and sweat. In reading his description, our own tears become mingled with Elder Whitney's and with the Savior's. Jesus' compassionate act moves us to compassion for him.

I know of a man, a genuinely good and compassionate man, a saintly soul and one of the great religious educators of our day, whose life was cut short by a brain tumor. He suffered considerable pain, and his family and friends felt much sorrow because of his relatively young age. In the midst of his suffering, the kind that comes with terminal cancer, he was asked by a colleague about his experience.

Through his tears he told of the difficult times but, more important, of the things he was learning through his suffering. He said that one of the great blessings that had come to him was the understanding he had gleaned about the Savior's suffering, especially the realization that if the Savior suffered as much as he did because he loved us, that was an awful lot of love.

When Brother West Belnap died, his example was extolled by Church leaders at the funeral. Today his picture hangs in one of the buildings on the Brigham Young University campus to remind those who know his story that the Savior does comprehend all the tears we weep because he wept them first. The Savior indeed descended below all things.

Another person I know was afflicted with a truly miserable condition that caused excruciating dizziness, nausea, and headaches and affected his ability to perform even the routine tasks of life. It was the type of malady that brings with it a special kind of emotional trauma—a longing for release, even through death, when the symptoms get really severe. There were times when he prayed for relief but felt none was forthcoming. What is worse, his suffering took on a spiritual dimension because he felt no Divine ear was listening.

Along with consulting doctors, the man also sought a priesthood blessing. In the midst of his suffering, my friend's father-in-law asked him if he had been administered to. Yes, was the reply.

The next question was, What did the blessing tell you? The man responded that the blessing told him that if he were patient, the illness would diminish, but more important, it would teach him lessons about the Savior's experience in Gethsemane that could be taught in no other way. His father-in-law, a man of great faith and wisdom, replied that that is what would indeed happen.

And so it has. Though the man at times felt like he was coming apart and would not want anyone to have to endure the malady he has endured, he knows through experience that pain and suffering are special teachers. As a result of his affliction, he now can say he has a deeper insight into what the Savior went through for all of Heavenly Father's children. The Savior went through that kind of suffering—and more—for he descended below all things.

As we contemplate our own trials and suffering, perhaps we can better appreciate another dimension of the Savior's experience in Gethsemane as he prayed the same prayer three times. Though he was the Father's Well Beloved Son, though the Father loved him with a perfect love, and though he prayed more earnestly each successive time, as Luke describes (Luke 22:44), there seemed to be no satisfactory answer. Each successive pleading with yet more intensity yielded no hoped-for result.

How like life for us this seems to be! I would be very

surprised to learn of someone who has never had at least one disappointment when it comes to the way prayers have been answered. And thus how grateful we ought to be for this dimension of the Savior's experience in Gethsemane—showing us again just how well he understands our plight. Doubt and disappointment come to all of us. I am told that President Hugh B. Brown used to say that no one comes to the position of authentic assurance without first having served an apprenticeship in doubt. Through his own experience, the Savior comprehends our mortal struggles and strivings.

Elder Rex D. Pinegar of the Seventy has summarized the lesson that emerges from Gethsemane about the need for patience in our prayers as we seek to follow the Lord's will in the midst of our trials:

> We can only try to imagine the anguish the Savior felt when we read in the Gospels that He was "sore amazed and very heavy" (Mark 14:33) that He "fell on his face" and prayed not once, but a second time, and then a third. (Matthew 26:39, 42, 44.) "Father, if thou be willing remove this cup from me: nevertheless not my will, but thine, be done." (Luke 22:42.). . . .
>
> Sometimes, when our prayers are not answered as we desire, we may feel the Lord has rejected us or that our prayer was in vain. We may begin to doubt our worthiness before God, or even the reality and power of prayer. That is when we must continue to pray with patience and faith and to listen for that peace. (*Church News*, 19 June 1999, 14)

## WITHDRAWAL OF LIGHT AND LIFE

Pain and suffering are powerful teachers. A wise man once said to me, "I learn the most when I hurt the worst!" Individuals among us have special empathy for the pain and suffering of others as well as the suffering experienced by the Savior because the pain they have endured has become a special teacher of divine principles.

Still, there is a huge difference between Jesus in Gethsemane and any other being on the earth, for the things any of us endure will never, ever compare to the Savior's sufferings or be compounded by the complete withdrawal of our Heavenly Father's Spirit and all heavenly influences from our lives, as was the Savior's lot. The withdrawal of the Father was a critical dimension of the Savior's incomprehensible agony in Gethsemane.

John 5:26 teaches that Jesus was a different kind of being from any of us. He had the powers, attributes, and characteristics of eternal life in the same way that our Heavenly Father possesses them. We are totally dependent upon Jesus Christ for these powers, but Jesus possessed them independently, having received them from his Father as part of his genetic makeup, as it were.

One gospel scholar has explained the ordeal in Gethsemane this way: "In order to satisfy the demands of divine justice and redeem fallen man, Christ sacrificed the attributes and powers of both physical and eternal life which He possessed on earth. In this way, Jesus made an 'infinite and eternal'—not merely a sinless human—sacrifice. To this end, the powers of eternal life or glory which He possessed were withdrawn, by His consent, as He commenced His great ordeal" (Andrus, *God, Man and the Universe*, 417).

His great ordeal commenced in Gethsemane. So great became this ordeal that Jesus pleaded with his Father three times to remove the cup. Brigham Young states that it was the withdrawal of our Heavenly Father from his Son, and hence the withdrawal of the spiritual powers of light and life in Gethsemane, that caused Jesus to sweat blood. President Young said, "If he [Jesus] had had the power of God upon him, he would not have sweat blood; but *all* was withdrawn from him, and a veil was cast over him" (*Journal of Discourses* 3:205–6; emphasis added).

Two conditions resulted from the withdrawal of the Father's power and influence and the powers of light and life from Jesus. First, he was engulfed by spiritual death and hell. Second, he became completely vulnerable to the powers of Satan.

## SATAN'S PRESENCE IN GETHSEMANE

The prophet Amulek warns us that when we fail to repent of our sins, we "become subjected to the spirit of the devil, and he doth seal you his; therefore, the Spirit of the Lord hath withdrawn from you, and hath no place in you, and *the devil hath all power over you*" (Alma 34:35; emphasis added).

Because we know that the power of God withdrew from Jesus, that he experienced the pains and sins of *all* people (Alma 7:11–13; D&C 18:11), and that he descended below *all* things and comprehends *all* things (D&C 88:6), we know that he faced the full power and rage of the devil, as Amulek said. Even Jesus, the greatest of all, did not escape Satan's wrath. Perhaps it would be more accurate to say *especially* Jesus did not escape

Satan's wrath. In other words, in Gethsemane Jesus became fully subject to the powers of Satan.

The experience of the Prophet Joseph Smith in the Sacred Grove helps us to understand, in small measure, what Jesus was subjected to and what he withstood in full measure in Gethsemane. The life of the one serves as a model or pattern for the other:

> After I had retired to the place where I had previously designed to go, having looked around me, and finding myself alone, I kneeled down and began to offer up the desires of my heart to God. I had scarcely done so, when immediately I was seized upon by some power which entirely overcame me, and had such an astonishing influence over me as to bind my tongue so that I could not speak. This darkness gathered around me, and it seemed to me for a time as if I were doomed to sudden destruction.
>
> But, exerting all my powers to call upon God to deliver me out of the power of this enemy which had seized upon me, and at the very moment when I was ready to sink into despair and abandon myself to destruction—not to an imaginary ruin, but to the power of some actual being from the unseen world, who had such marvelous power as I had never before felt in any being—just at this moment of great alarm, I saw a pillar of light exactly over my head, above the brightness of the sun, which descended gradually until it fell upon me.
>
> It no sooner appeared than I found myself delivered

from the enemy which held me bound. (Joseph Smith–History 1:15–17)

Joseph Smith learned that the powers of darkness and Satan's control over the elements, as well as his attempts to control the physical bodies of mortals, are real. Jesus endured these same powers but to an even greater degree—in fact, the greatest degree possible. In the case of Jesus, however, unlike that of Joseph Smith, there was no ultimate deliverance by heavenly beings from Satan's complete fury. Of the Savior's experience, President Boyd K. Packer said: "He, by choice, accepted the penalty for all mankind for the sum total of all wickedness and depravity. . . . In choosing, He faced the awesome power of the evil one who was not confined to flesh nor subject to mortal pain. That was Gethsemane" (*Ensign*, May 1988, 69).

Thus, we may say with perfect accuracy as well as irony that while (or maybe because) our Heavenly Father was not present in the Garden of Gethsemane that awful night almost two thousand years ago, we know that someone else was—Satan. He was there, hurling at Jesus every horror of which he was capable, trying to force the Savior to retreat from, renounce, and forfeit his redemptive mission.

The truth is chilling. Unspeakable horror was at work that night in Gethsemane, when eternity hung in the balance. But Jesus came off conqueror against the evil one, whose presence was very real. Elder Talmage has penned the scene for us in memorable language:

> Christ's agony in the garden is unfathomable by the finite mind, both as to intensity and cause. . . . He struggled and groaned under a burden such as no other

being who has lived on earth might even conceive as possible. It was not physical pain, nor mental anguish alone, that caused Him to suffer such torture as to produce an extrusion of blood from every pore; but a spiritual agony of soul such as only God was capable of experiencing. No other man, however great his powers of physical or mental endurance, could have suffered so; for his human organism would have succumbed, and syncope would have produced unconsciousness and welcome oblivion. In that hour of anguish Christ met and *overcame all the horrors that Satan, "the prince of this world" could inflict* [John 14:30]. The frightful struggle incident to the temptations immediately following the Lord's baptism was surpassed and overshadowed by this supreme contest with the powers of evil. (*Jesus the Christ*, 613; emphasis added)

The unimaginable happened in Gethsemane. Jesus Christ, the greatest of all, the one perfect Being who walked the earth, the all-powerful God of the Old Testament, was turned over to the buffetings of Satan. Truly, he descended below all things.

## TEMPTATION

From all that has been written in scripture and taught by prophets, it appears that Gethsemane entailed risk. The Savior's experience in the garden was not without danger. One of Satan's roles is the great tempter. And he unleashed all his power on Jesus.

To those who may think Jesus' station prevented him from being able to experience real risk, real temptation, we simply point out King Benjamin's prophecy: "And lo, he shall suffer temptations, and pain of body, hunger, thirst, and fatigue, even more than man can suffer, except it be unto death; for behold, blood cometh from every pore, so great shall be his anguish for the wickedness and the abominations of his people" (Mosiah 3:7).

Here we have it. The omnipotent God of the universe would, for a time, shed his status and power and condescend to come to earth. He would, as the word *condescend* literally means, "come down with" the people to suffer far more than any human could withstand and not succumb to death— including temptations of every kind. He would experience these temptations to such an extent that justice could not say, "You really didn't know what it means to be human."

We are indebted to C. S. Lewis (1899–1963) for providing us with a most magnificent insight into the Savior's temptation and atoning experience:

> No man knows how bad he is till he has tried very hard to be good. A silly idea is current that good people do not know what temptation means. This is an obvious lie. Only those who try to resist temptation know how strong it is; after all, you find out the strength of the German army by fighting against it, not by giving in. You find out the strength of a wind by trying to walk against it, not by lying down. A man who gives into temptation after five minutes simply does not know what it would have been like an hour later.
>
> That is why bad people in one sense know very little about badness. They've always lived a sheltered life by always giving in. We never find out the strength of the

evil impulse inside us until we try to fight it: and Christ, because he was the only man who never yielded to temptation, is also the only man who knows to the full what temptation means—the only complete realist. (*Mere Christianity*, 126)

This is a stunning revelation, not to mention an irony of staggering proportions. Jesus was severely tempted—tested to the limit because he was the greatest of all. For him, as for us, some of his greatest tests came as he was tempted: on the Mount of Temptation east of the Jericho Valley, on the pinnacle of the Temple in Jerusalem, and in the Garden of Gethsemane on the Mount of Olives. For him, as for us, the tests and temptations are all part of Heavenly Father's plan and purposes. As finite beings we cannot know the mind of God in all things, but we can pay attention to his prophets, who give us glimpses of the eternal perspective.

President Brigham Young knew something of the tests and temptations Jesus faced relative to the tests and temptations all of us face. Jesus was tempted and tested and had to confront the enemy of all righteousness in direct proportion to the light and truth he possessed. He said:

> Is there a reason for men and women being exposed more constantly and more powerfully, to the power of the enemy, by having visions than by not having them? There is and it is simply this—God never bestows upon His people, or upon an individual, superior blessings without a severe trial to prove them, to prove that individual, or that people to see whether they will keep their covenants with Him, and keep in remembrance what He has shown them. Then the greater the vision,

the greater the display of the power of the enemy. And when such individuals are off their guard they are left to themselves, as Jesus was. (*Journal of Discourses,* 3:205–6)

Jesus was tempted in direct proportion to the light and life given him. Each of us is similarly tested and tempted. But that is good news. As one man expressed in the midst of life's trials, "The Lord allows it because he thinks you're worth it."

In light of King Benjamin's prophecy, C. S. Lewis's insight, and President Young's comment, I believe it is possible to resist the less noble impulses inside us and the greater temptations that surround us. That is, we can "overcome by faith" (D&C 76:53), or, more specifically, overcome temptation through our faith in Jesus Christ (Alma 37:33).

Jesus knows our challenges. He understands them even better than we do, precisely because he resisted the tempter to the very end. Our sons and daughters must know from us that it is possible for them to call upon a true Friend and find help in time of need. They can resist the evil impulses planted in their hearts by the evil one. We may expect it of them because of their standing and station and because of our confidence in them after they have been properly taught.

Apostles and prophets have taught that members of the house of Israel living in this last dispensation are spirit children of our Father in Heaven who have been reserved to be born at this time because of their strength and talents.

Speaking to members of the Church, President Gordon B. Hinckley said, "You are a great generation. . . . I think you are the best generation who have ever lived in this Church"

(*Church News*, 14 February 1998, 4). Elder Neal A. Maxwell noted that

> there is the increasing presence of choice and talent-laden spirits sent now because of what each can add to the symphony of salvation. President George Q. Cannon said these were reserved because they would have "the courage and determination to face the world" and because they would "honor" God "supremely" and would be "fearless" and "obedient" to God "under all cir-cumstances." I am impressed, deeply impressed, with the youth and young adults in the Church, collectively. President Cannon's statement simply underscores, prophetically, what so many of us see and feel in this regard (*Deposition of a Disciple*, 63–64).

## EFFECT ON THE APOSTLES

We know from Matthew's account that Jesus was concerned for the welfare of his special witnesses during the entire time they were with him in the Garden of Gethsemane. At least twice he went to them to instruct them to watch and pray so as not to enter into temptation (Matthew 26:40–44). We also know that his concern was well founded. It was not just because of his own personal experience with Satan in the garden that he was concerned. Rather, as we come to learn, Satan was already filling the minds of the apostles with doubt, anger, and frustration over Jesus' actions in the garden.

In the Joseph Smith Translation of Mark 14:36–38, which is significantly different from the King James Version, we see how Satan had already begun his work among the apostles:

And they came to a place which was named Gethsemane, which was a garden; and the disciples began to
be sore amazed, and to be very heavy, and to complain
in their hearts, wondering if this be the Messiah.

And Jesus knowing their hearts, said to his disciples,
Sit ye here, while I shall pray.

And he taketh with him, Peter, and James, and
John, and rebuked them, and said unto them, My soul is
exceeding sorrowful, even unto death; tarry ye here and
watch.

From this passage we understand that the apostles had
begun to question whether Jesus really was the Messiah. We
may imagine that the more Jesus suffered, the more the apostles
doubted his messianic identity. After all, *the* King-Messiah, in
the minds of most Jews, was not supposed to suffer, not supposed
to fail in restoring the great Davidic kingdom of ancient times,
not supposed to collapse under the weight of spiritual distress
nor retreat in the face of expectations of great demonstrations
of power, signs, and wonders.

Obviously, the apostles did not fully comprehend the true
and varied roles of the real Messiah. In their minds he was
supposed to be the unfailing and triumphant warrior-
conqueror-deliverer who would restore again the kingdom of
Israel—an expectation the apostles still held even at the time
of the Savior's ascension (Acts 1:6). And this was their
Achilles' heel, so to speak, which Satan worked on. That is
why the Savior was so concerned for their welfare that night
in Gethsemane and why he repeatedly asked them to pray and
watch so as not to enter into temptation, or rather, even
greater temptations.

Joseph Smith's translation of Mark 14 does not contradict the truth of the King James Version, which tells us that *Jesus* began to be sore amazed and very heavy. But the Joseph Smith Translation rendering does give us a more complete perspective on Gethsemane. It shows us what was happening in the minds and hearts of the apostles (they were, in a very limited sense, suffering with their Master), while the King James Version tells us what was happening at the same time to the Savior in the garden as a result of the great turmoil and spiritual onslaught that engulfed him. Both the Joseph Smith Translation account and the King James Version account are true. Both are incredibly valuable. Both teach us what happened in Gethsemane.

## TOWARD GOLGOTHA

After Jesus had wrestled for some time (exactly how long we do not know) with the forces of evil and the onslaught of pain, sin, sorrow, and suffering and after he had descended below *all* things, the intensity of his experience seems to have subsided somewhat. He finished praying for the third time that his Father would remove the bitter cup, but coming to know with absolute certainty that his Father's will was otherwise, he drank the cup he was given and then returned to his apostles, who were sound asleep: "Then cometh he to his disciples, and saith unto them, Sleep on now, and take your rest: behold, the hour is at hand, and the Son of man is betrayed into the hands of sinners" (Matthew 26:45).

In Gethsemane, the ancient prophecies of the Savior's solitary suffering were fulfilled. As the psalmist noted a thousand years before the actual events of Gethsemane occurred, the Savior would find no support from his apostolic associates as he suffered: "Reproach hath broken my heart; and I am full of heaviness: and I looked for some to take pity, but there was none; and for comforters, but I found none" (Psalm 69:20).

Even though we have been made aware of the apostles' weaknesses, it is still wise for us to regard them with the highest respect and deference. These were great men, among the very best on the earth at that or any other time in history. They were *special* witnesses. They had given up everything in pursuit of their Master's call to follow him. In some cases, they had consecrated a significant amount. By the time they reached Gethsemane that awful night, they had been awake for many hours straight, and, above all, they were mortals subject to all the influences and frailties of mortality as brought on by the Fall.

They were also leaders in transition. Nothing like the events they had witnessed and participated in had ever happened before, nor would the events that followed over the course of the next three days find any precedent in the history of our universe. All the events of the meridian dispensation were as new to the members of the Quorum of the Twelve then as the events of this final dispensation were to Joseph Smith and his associates. We ought therefore to increase our gratitude for the strength and power demonstrated by Jesus' original Quorum of the Twelve rather than seek to multiply their shortcomings.

For Jesus, there was more to be endured. By his own admission, the bitter cup was not yet finished. The arrest in the garden, the arraignment before Jewish as well as Roman leaders, the suffering, torture, scourging, and mockery at the hands of wicked and ignorant men, and ultimately crucifixion itself—all these lay ahead of Jesus after he finished that special ordeal that was Gethsemane. Not surprisingly, the very same apostles who had been infected by doubt tried to keep him from the suffering that lay ahead. Jesus rebuked them by reminding them that the bitter cup had not yet been completely consumed. Would they now intervene to try to prevent the final acts from unfolding as God the Father desired? "Then said Jesus unto Peter, Put up thy sword into the sheath: the cup which my Father hath given me, shall I not drink it?" (John 18:11).

The final act was played out. Jesus drained the dregs of the bitter cup, and the eternal possibilities of Heavenly Father's children were safely secured.

*Therefore I command you to repent—repent, lest I smite you by the rod of my mouth, and by my wrath, and by my anger, and your sufferings be sore—how sore you know not, how exquisite you know not, yea, how hard to bear you know not.*

*For behold, I, God, have suffered these things for all, that they might not suffer if they would repent;*

*But if they would not repent they must suffer even as I;*

*Which suffering caused myself, even God, the greatest of all, to tremble because of pain, and to bleed at every pore, and to suffer both body and spirit—and would that I might not drink the bitter cup, and shrink—*

*Nevertheless, glory be to the Father, and I partook and finished my preparations unto the children of men.*

DOCTRINE AND COVENANTS 19:15–19

# CHAPTER 6

# The Savior's Testimony of the Bitter Cup

Significantly, it was not his arrest, trial, or crucifixion that Jesus recounted to others with vivid recollection after his resurrection. It was the bitter cup in Gethsemane. President Joseph Fielding Smith helps us to understand why this is so:

> It is understood by many that the great suffering of Jesus Christ came through the driving of nails in His hands and in His feet, and in being suspended upon a cross, until death mercifully released Him. That is not the case. As excruciating, as severe as was that punishment, . . . yet still greater was the suffering which He endured in carrying the burdens of the sins of the world—my sins, and your sins, and the sins of every living creature. This suffering came before He ever got to the cross, and it caused the blood to come forth from the pores of His body, so great was the anguish of His soul, the torment of His spirit that He was called upon to undergo. (Conference Report, April 1944, 50)

Gethsemane seems to have so affected the Savior that he reminded his audiences of it when he spoke to them at the beginning of two new dispensations after his resurrection. The first was in the Americas in A.D. 34, and the next was also in the Americas, when the Savior spoke to Joseph Smith in March 1830 (D&C 19).

The Book of Mormon records the feelings of the twenty-five hundred Nephites assembled at the temple in Bountiful and then the powerful words of the Savior to them:

> And it came to pass, as they understood they cast their eyes up again towards heaven; and behold, they saw a Man descending out of heaven; and he was clothed in a white robe; and he came down and stood in the midst of them; and the eyes of the whole multitude were turned upon him, and they durst not open their mouths, even one to another, and wist not what it meant, for they thought it was an angel that had appeared unto them.
>
> And it came to pass that he stretched forth his hand and spake unto the people, saying:
>
> Behold, I am Jesus Christ, whom the prophets testified shall come into the world.
>
> And behold, I am the light and the life of the world; and I have drunk out of that bitter cup which the Father hath given me, and have glorified the Father in taking upon me the sins of the world, in the which I have suffered the will of the Father in all things from the beginning. (3 Nephi 11:8–11)

Thus the Savior reminds his disciples, then and now, that his consumption of the bitter cup was indeed the fulfillment of his promise made to the Father long ago, in the very beginning, that he would suffer the will of the Father in *all* things. We are reminded of the Great Council in Heaven, held during our premortal existence, when the Firstborn said, "Father, thy will be done, and the glory be thine forever" (Moses 4:2). Gethsemane and Calvary are the two places where Jesus fulfilled his promise and accomplished the will of the Father.

Just as the Savior remembers Gethsemane, so should we always remember it. It has remained a focal point of his self-identification. But neither of Christ's postresurrection accounts of the bitter cup (3 Nephi 11; D&C 19) was given to scare us into submission nor to force our obedience. Rather, I think a very earnest Savior is trying to tell us just exactly what it cost to ransom us from the grasp of justice, what price was paid to secure our freedom from death, hell, and the devil.

## THE PRICE OF REDEMPTION

Occasionally mortals indulge in "what if . . ." speculations about certain events. "What if this would have happened instead of that?" Sometimes the answers are useless. But there are other times when the conjured possibilities can teach profound lessons. In the case of the Savior's redemptive acts, a prophet in the Book of Mormon helps us to see the frightening truth about our human plight if there had been no Gethsemane and no Calvary. Without the Savior's atoning sacrifice, we would have had no escape from the awful grasp of death, hell, and the devil. In fact, without both Gethsemane and Calvary, each of us would have become devils, just like Lucifer himself in his irredeemable condition. Jacob says:

Wherefore, it must needs be an infinite atonement—

save it should be an infinite atonement this corruption could not put on incorruption. Wherefore, the first judgment which came upon man must needs have remained to an endless duration. And if so, this flesh must have laid down to rot and to crumble to its mother earth, to rise no more.

O the wisdom of God, his mercy and grace! For behold, if the flesh should rise no more our spirits must become subject to that angel who fell from before the presence of the Eternal God, and became the devil, to rise no more.

And our spirits must have become like unto him, and we become devils, angels to a devil, to be shut out from the presence of our God, and to remain with the father of lies, in misery, like unto himself; yea, to that being who beguiled our first parents, who transformeth himself nigh unto an angel of light, and stirreth up the children of men unto secret combinations of murder and all manner of secret works of darkness. (2 Nephi 9:7–9)

In declaring the explicit cost of our redemption from the throes of sin as well as the devil, the Savior's personal testimony in Doctrine and Covenants 19:18 is without parallel. God himself, the greatest of all, one of three all-knowing and all-powerful Gods in the entire universe, *trembled* because of pain, *bled* at every pore, suffered *body and spirit* to rescue us. The pain that he suffered was "the pain of all men" (D&C 18:11). When he said he "suffered these things for all" he was not exaggerating. He meant it. He suffered the consequences of *every* sin committed by Adam and by all of Adam's posterity. He suffered both physically and spiritually. He suffered to the very limits of possibility. There is no way or manner in which he did not suffer. He suffered everything imaginable. He suffered for billions and billions of lifetimes of sin and sorrow. There is not anyone for whom he did not suffer. "The Savior's Atonement is stunningly inclusive," said Sister Sheri L. Dew. "Come one, come all, the Lord has invited. The gospel of Jesus Christ is for every man and woman, boy and girl. He doesn't change the rules for the rich or the poor, the married or unmarried, the Portuguese or the Chinese. The gospel is for *every one* of us, and the spiritual requirements and rewards are universal. In matters pertaining to salvation, '*all* are alike unto God' (2 Ne. 26:33, emphasis added)" (*Ensign*, May 1999, 66).

## SUFFERING AND CONTRADICTION

Though the Savior's suffering is for all individuals, ironically he suffered alone. He said on several occasions, "I have trodden the wine-press alone, and have brought judgment upon all people; and none were with me" (D&C 133:50; D&C 76:107; 88:106; Revelation 14:20). The metaphor of the winepress is appropriate because the image it conjures up takes us immediately to the Garden of Gethsemane where, still today, we can see remnants of ancient winepresses.

Anciently, winepresses and olive presses were sometimes used interchangeably. Several people would get into the press, a rock-lined pit with a mosaic or plaster floor, and, holding onto one another, smash the grapes or olives with their feet until the fruit turned into a thick pulp. Unless one held onto others in the press, it was almost impossible to lift one's feet in the thick sludge to tromp the grapes into juice. It also became very slippery, and without others in the press to hang onto for support, it was very easy to fall. Thus, when the Savior says he trod the winepress alone, he means that at a certain point in Gethsemane no one was there to help him through his ordeal. Ironically, in a place named for an activity that required several participants, one Man suffered for all men—the greatest contradiction in the history of created things.

From what has been revealed to us, we cannot help but believe that a significant source of Jesus' great spiritual agony stemmed from the total contradiction of the situation. In Gethsemane, God, the greatest of all, suffered the greatest contradictions of all. As we have said, the Prophet Joseph Smith taught that Jesus Christ "descended in suffering below that which man can suffer; or, in other words, suffered greater sufferings, and was exposed to *more powerful contradictions* than any man can be. But, notwithstanding all this, he kept the law of God, and remained without sin, showing thereby that it is in the power of man to keep the law and remain without sin" (*Lectures on Faith*, 5:2). This has to be one of the great principles of mortality. We, like Jesus, suffer contradictions as part of our probation on this earth; there is no doubt of that. It is what we do in the face of those contradictions, how we react, that demonstrates our commitment to God and thus determines our place in eternity.

All of the noble and great leaders among our Father's children have experienced such contradictions in their lives. Perhaps the most notable, besides the Savior, is Abraham. He was commanded to offer Isaac, his long-promised son, as a human sacrifice, even though Isaac was the son through whom Abraham believed he was to receive God's promises of innumerable posterity and an everlasting line of priesthood holders. Moreover, God abhorred human sacrifice, and Abraham himself had been rescued from becoming a human sacrifice under his own father's hand by the very same Deity who then turned around and commanded Abraham to sacrifice his son (Abraham 1:5–16).

As Abraham learned, the contradictions of mortality serve a great purpose. Not only do they act as the Lord's refining fire but they precede great and marvelous blessings. Said Moroni, a prophet who knew a great deal about trials, tribulations, and contradictions: "Ye receive no witness until after the trial of your faith" (Ether 12:6). We can state the principle in another way: the greater the contradiction, faithfully endured, the greater the blessing enjoyed afterward.

Again, Abraham is a good example. Because of Abraham's faithfulness, God made good on every promise to him, and more. His son Isaac has the honor of being one of only two individuals designated "only begotten son" (Hebrews 11:17). The other is Jesus Christ. Because of Abraham's faithfulness, his experience with Isaac on Mount Moriah is held up as *the* earthly model of the relationship that existed between God the Father and his Only Begotten Son. "Behold, they believed in Christ and worshiped the Father in his name, and also we worship the Father in his name. And for this intent we keep the law of Moses, it pointing our souls to him; and for this cause it is sanctified unto us for righteousness, even as it was accounted unto Abraham in the wilderness to be obedient unto the commands of God in offering up his son Isaac, *which is a similitude of God and his Only Begotten Son*" (Jacob 4:5; emphasis added). And ultimately, because of Abraham's faithfulness, he and his sons "have entered into their exaltation, according to the promises, and sit upon thrones, and are not angels but are gods" (D&C 132:37).

Every disciple of the Lord and true follower of Abraham

will face the kind of tests, trials, and contradictions the great patriarch faced. These will be different for every person, but they will come! The Lord has said, "They [those who profess discipleship] must needs be chastened and tried, even as Abraham, who was commanded to offer up his only son. For all those who will not endure chastening, but deny me, cannot be sanctified" (D&C 101:4–5).

Abraham is the standard. He was true and faithful to Jehovah, and his life became a powerful witness of the principle that "after much tribulation . . . cometh the blessing" (D&C 103:12).

So it is for each one of us. We remember that the Lord said "after *much* tribulation cometh the blessing," not a little difficulty or a small challenge here and there. President John Taylor said, "You will have all kinds of trials to pass through. And it is quite as necessary for you to be tried as it was for Abraham and other men of God. . . . God will feel after you, and He will take hold of you and wrench your very heart strings, and if you cannot stand it you will not be fit for an inheritance in the Celestial Kingdom of God" (*Journal of Discourses*, 24:197).

All such tests are calculated to allow us the opportunity to demonstrate our loyalty just as Abraham demonstrated his. God doesn't want anything but our minds, our hearts, and all that we possess! He does not want much—he wants everything. And he desires with all his soul to give us back everything he possesses. We are asked to give up all in order to receive an infinitely greater all.

The magnitude of the promise is almost incomprehensible and the unevenness of the offer staggering: everything we possess in exchange for everything God possesses! Why would any of us be unwilling to sacrifice all we have been given, all that is not even ours to begin with? I treasure the words of President George Q. Cannon:

> There is no sacrifice that God can ask of us or His servants whom He has chosen to lead us that we should hesitate about making. In one sense of the word it is no sacrifice. We may call it so because it comes in contact with our selfishness and our unbelief; but it ought not to come in contact with our faith. . . .
>
> Why did the Lord ask such things of Abraham? Because, knowing what his future would be and that he would be the father of an innumerable posterity, he was determined to test him. God did not do this for His own sake for He knew by His foreknowledge what Abraham would do; but the purpose was to impress upon Abraham a lesson and to enable him to attain unto knowledge that he could not obtain in any other way. That is why God tries all of us. It is not for His own knowledge, for He knows all things beforehand. He knows all your lives and everything you will do. But he tries us for our own good, that we may know ourselves; for it is most important that a man should know himself. He required Abraham to submit to this trial because He intended to give him glory, exaltation and honor. He intended to make him a king and a priest, to share with Himself the glory, power and dominion which He exercised. (*Gospel Truth*, 89)

With regard to the principle of contradictions, as in all things, Jesus is our greatest exemplar, particularly in that awful night in Gethsemane. When it comes to contradiction, Abraham on Mount Moriah and Jesus in Gethsemane are like each other, but Gethsemane involved so much more. The Jewish people refer to Mount Moriah as the place of infinite resignation, because Abraham resigned himself to follow God's will even in the face of overwhelming contradiction. It can be justly said that Gethsemane was the night of infinite resignation, infinite suffering, *and* infinite contradiction.

Perhaps it was the night of infinite suffering *because* of infinite contradiction. Though Jesus was the Son of the Highest, in Gethsemane he descended below all things. Though he was sent out of love (John 3:16) and though he was characterized as the embodiment of love (1 John 4:8), in Gethsemane he was surrounded by hate and betrayal. Though he was the light and life of the world, in Gethsemane he was subjected to darkness and spiritual death. Though he was sinless, in Gethsemane he was weighed down by monumental sin and iniquity. Though he gave no offense in anything (2 Corinthians 6:3), in Gethsemane he suffered for the offenses of all. In Gethsemane, the sinless One became the great sinner (2 Corinthians 5:21), that is, he experienced fully the plight of sinners. Though he was fully deserving of the Father's love and the Father's glory, in Gethsemane he suffered the wrath of Almighty God.

Is it any wonder, then, that the Savior said to Joseph Smith that unrepentant sinners would be smitten by his own wrath, by his anger, by sufferings so sore, exquisite, and hard to bear they could not be comprehended? He himself had suffered these things, and if individuals will not accept his suffering, then they must suffer those same things themselves.

The contradictions of Gethsemane filled the bitter cup. In contemplating them, how can we fail to be moved to tears of gratitude because the Savior drank the cup to its dregs and made it possible for us to escape the kind of suffering demanded by the exacting requirements of justice? But there is another reason for gratitude.

We know that even with the benefits of the Atonement fully operating in our lives, mortality still entails some suffering and some contradictions for each of us. Yet, because the Savior endured perfectly his staggering contradictions, we will be recompensed for our own faithful endurance of life's contradictions, injustices, and flat-out unfair circumstances. That is, through the Atonement, all of life's contradictions, all injustices, and all unfair circumstances will be made up to us, all unfair disadvantages will be made right in the eternal scheme of things. In an ironic twist, because of Christ's atonement, because of his supreme act of mercy which rescues us from the demands of justice, justice ultimately becomes our friend by making up to us for all of the things in life that weren't fair and right. All unfair circumstances and contradictions will be put right—if we remain faithful to the Savior.

## LIFE'S TUTORS

President Spencer W. Kimball was a man acquainted with many of life's trials, contradictions, and injustices. I appreciate his counsel because he lived it. He intimated that if mortality were the absolute beginning and end of our existence, then sorrow, suffering, pain, unfairness, injustice, and failure would be the greatest calamities. But mortality is only a very small fraction of eternity. In Gethsemane and on the cross, the Savior turned sorrow, pain, and injustice into the ultimate blessing for us by making possible eternal life. In fact, the Savior's experience in Gethsemane showed us how suffering can become one of our great tutors. President Kimball said (in *Tragedy or Destiny*, 3):

Being human, we would expel from our lives physical pain and mental anguish and assure ourselves of continual ease and comfort, but if we were to close the
doors upon sorrow and distress, we might be excluding
our greatest friends and benefactors. Suffering can make
saints of people as they learn patience, long-suffering,
and self-mastery. The sufferings of our Savior were part
of his education. "Though he were a Son, yet learned he
obedience by the things which he suffered; And being
made perfect, he became the author of eternal salvation
unto all them that obey him" (Hebrews 5:8–9).

I love the verse of "How Firm a Foundation"—

When through the deep waters I call thee to go,
The rivers of sorrow shall not thee o'erflow
For I will be with thee, thy troubles to bless,
And sanctify to thee thy deepest distress.
(*Hymns*, [1985, no. 85])

The Savior is a true friend, and because of his experience in
Gethsemane, our trials and contradictions also turn out to be
our friends and special tutors. His atonement makes eternal
existence, bathed in a fulness of joy, a reality. Our own experiences, the enjoyable as well as the distasteful, become the foundation of our quest for knowledge and help us to become more
like our Heavenly Parents. As Elder Orson F. Whitney said:

No pain that we suffer, no trial that we experience
is wasted. It ministers to our education, to the develop-
ment of such qualities as patience, faith, fortitude
and humility. All that we suffer and all that we endure,
especially when we endure it patiently, builds up our

characters, purifies our hearts, expands our souls, and makes us more tender and charitable, more worthy to be called the children of God . . . and it is through sorrow and suffering, toil and tribulation, that we gain the education that we come here to acquire and which will make us more like our Father and Mother in heaven. (In Kimball, *Tragedy or Destiny,* 4)

Each of us experiences something of Gethsemane in our own lives. We suffer contradictions and injustices and feel pain for others as well as experience pain because of the actions of others. Sometimes we may even feel we are having to endure our own Gethsemane. But the Savior is able to cure all the hurt and heal all the bruises and in the process transforms our trials, tribulations, and sufferings into sacred experiences.

President James E. Faust, a counselor in the First Presidency, gave this instructive counsel:

At times I have stumbled and been less than I should have been. All of us experience those wrenching, defining, difficult decisions that move us to a higher level of spirituality. They are the Gethsemanes of our lives that bring with them great pain and anguish. Sometimes they are too sacred to be shared publicly. They are the watershed experiences that help purge us of our unrighteous desires for the things of the world. As the scales of worldliness are taken from our eyes, we see more clearly who we are and what our responsibilities are concerning our divine destiny. (*Ensign,* November 2000, 59)

Our obedience and sacrifice in the face of trials and tribulations allow us to come to know God in a more intimate way than we could have known him without our sufferings. The historian George Bancroft, when reflecting upon a low point for George Washington and the patriots during the American Revolution, wrote words that apply to all of us: "The spirit of the Most High dwells among the afflicted, rather than the prosperous; and he who has never broken his bread in tears knows not the heavenly powers" (in Dibble, "Delivered by the Power of God," 48).

Indeed, righteous persons who seem to have suffered the most also seem to appreciate their suffering the most and learn what God wants his children to learn from their sacrifice and suffering in obedience. In addition to Abraham and other scriptural figures are individuals from Latter-day Saint history who allowed their sacrifices and sufferings to tutor them. A powerful lesson was taught by one of the survivors of the Martin handcart company when, years later, he heard criticism leveled against Church leaders for allowing the handcart company to take its journey in such adverse conditions. In a session of general conference, Elder James E. Faust recounted that the man said:

> "I ask you to stop this criticism. You are discussing a matter you know nothing about. Cold historic facts mean nothing here, for they give no proper interpretation of the questions involved. Mistake to send the Handcart Company out so late in the season? Yes. But I was in that company and my wife was in it and Sister Nellie Unthank whom you have cited was there, too. We suffered beyond anything you can imagine and many died of exposure and starvation, but did you ever hear a survivor of that company utter a word of criticism? *Not one of that company ever apostatized or left the*

*Church, because every one of us came through with the absolute knowledge that God lives for we became acquainted with him in our extremities.*

"I have pulled my handcart when I was so weak and weary from illness and lack of food that I could hardly put one foot ahead of the other. I have looked ahead and seen a patch of sand or a hill slope and I have said, I can go only that far and there I must give up, for I cannot pull the load through it. . . .

"I have gone on to that sand and when I reached it, the cart began pushing me. I have looked back many times to see who was pushing my cart, but my eyes saw no one. I knew then that the angels of God were there.

"Was I sorry that I chose to come by handcart? No. Neither then nor any minute of my life since. *The price we paid to become acquainted with God was a privilege to pay, and I am thankful that I was privileged to come in the Martin Handcart Company.*" (*Relief Society Magazine,* Jan. 1948, p. 8.)

Here then is a great truth. In the pain, the agony, and the heroic endeavors of life, we pass through a refiner's fire, and the insignificant and the unimportant in our lives can melt away like dross and make our faith bright, intact, and strong. In this way the divine image can be mirrored from the soul. It is part of the purging toll exacted of some to become acquainted with God. In the agonies of life, we seem to listen better to the faint, godly whisperings of the Divine Shepherd. (*Ensign,* May 1979, 53)

Sacrifice and obedience to God's will in the face of trials, tribulations, and suffering are the price we pay to know God! We are never more like the Savior than when we offer our obedience in the face of affliction. Even the sacrifices we think we are making for righteousness' sake are rewarded with the blessings of eternal life and everlasting happiness precisely because of the Savior's own sacrifice in Gethsemane and on the cross of Calvary. Everything we suffer and sacrifice for righteousness' sake will be made up to us because of the Savior's suffering and sacrifice. The Prophet Joseph Smith taught: "All your losses will be made up to you in the resurrection; provided you continue faithful. By the vision of the Almighty I have seen it" (*Teachings of the Prophet Joseph Smith*, 296).

I am reminded that our English word *sacrifice* derives from a combination of two Latin words, *sacer* ("sacred") and *facere* ("to make"), thus meaning "to make sacred." Of course, *sacred* means "set apart for or dedicated to Deity." Does the Savior's sacrifice in Gethsemane and on Golgotha mean, then, that we are set apart for God's use, for his purposes? Or that we have been dedicated and singled out to become like God? Or does it mean something else? Any way we look at it, Jesus' experience in Gethsemane has something to do with the answer. His life is bound up with ours, inescapably.

## WHAT HE ASKS OF US

Ultimately, the Savior's personal testimony regarding the bitter cup seems strikingly simple in its intention—to help us understand what it cost him to remove the burden of our sins and to teach us what is required for us to be able to enjoy his rich gift. Repentance! Of all things he could have asked, he asks us to repent. He asks us to change, to turn to him, to leave our sins and misdeeds behind and commit to trying with all our hearts to live good and decent lives. He wants to spare us the suffering he experienced. He desires only *our* welfare.

In an early revelation of this dispensation, the Lord instructed his servants Joseph Smith, Oliver Cowdery, and others to "say nothing but repentance unto this generation" (D&C 6:9). Interestingly, the Lord followed his own counsel when he bore witness of his experience in Gethsemane, as recorded in Doctrine and Covenants 19:15–19, for there he too focused on repentance.

Repentance is sometimes misunderstood. In a powerful address at Brigham Young University, Elder Theodore M. Burton explained the doctrine of repentance in a most helpful fashion:

> Just what *is* repentance? Actually it is easier for me to tell you what repentance is *not* than to tell you what repentance *is*.
>
> My present assignment as a General Authority is to assist the First Presidency. I prepare information for them to use in considering applications to readmit transgressors into the Church and to restore priesthood and/or temple blessings. Many times a bishop will write: "I feel he has suffered enough!" But suffering is not repentance. Suffering comes from *lack* of complete repentance. A stake president will write: "I feel he has been punished enough!" But punishment is not repentance. Punishment *follows* disobedience and *precedes* repentance. A husband will write: "My wife has confessed everything!" But confession is not repentance. Confession is an admission of guilt that occurs *as* repentance begins. A wife will write: "My husband is filled

with remorse!" But remorse is not repentance. Remorse and sorrow continue because a person has *not* yet fully repented. But if suffering, punishment, confession, remorse, and sorrow are not repentance, what *is* repentance? ("Meaning of Repentance," 96)

Elder Burton explained that repentance is a doctrine discussed with clarity in the Old Testament. *Repentance* is the English word used to translate the Hebrew word *shuv*, which means "to turn, return, or turn back." Elder Burton then quoted Ezekiel:

"When I say unto the wicked, O wicked man, thou shalt surely die; if thou dost not speak to warn the wicked from his way, that wicked man shall die in his iniquity; but his blood will I require at thine hand.

"Nevertheless, if thou warn the wicked of his way to [*shuv*; or] turn from it; if he do not [*shuv*; or] turn from his way, he shall die in his iniquity; but thou hast delivered thy soul.

"Therefore, O thou son of man, speak unto the house of Israel; Thus ye speak, saying, If our transgressions and our sins be upon us, and we pine away in them, how should we then live?

"Say unto them, As I live, saith the Lord God, I have no pleasure in the death of the wicked; but that the wicked [*shuv*; or] turn from his way and live: [*shuv, shuv!*] turn ye, turn ye from your evil ways; for why will ye die, O house of Israel?" (Ezek. 33:8–11)

I know of no kinder, sweeter passage in the Old Testament than those beautiful lines. Can you hear a kind, wise, gentle, loving Father in Heaven pleading with you to [shuv] or turn back to him, to leave unhappiness, sorrow, regret, and despair behind and now turn back to your Father's family where you can find happiness, joy, and acceptance among his other children? In the Father's family, you are surrounded with love and affection. That is the message of the Old Testament, and prophet after prophet writes of [shuv], which is that turning back to the family of the Lord where you can be received with joy and rejoicing. . . .

People must somehow be made to realize that the true meaning of repentance is that we do not require people to be punished or to punish themselves, but to change their lives so they can escape eternal punishment. If they have this understanding, it will relieve their anxiety and fears and become a welcome and treasured word in our religious vocabulary. ("Meaning of Repentance," 96–97)

True repentance requires that we turn to God, change our sinful ways, confess our sins, renew our pledge or covenant with the Lord, repay our debt, serve others, and never return to our iniquity. To the Prophet Joseph Smith, the Lord said: "Behold, he who has repented of his sins, the same is forgiven, and I, the Lord, remember them no more. By this ye may know if a man repenteth of his sins—behold, he will confess them and forsake them" (D&C 58:42–43).

One element of repentance that we sometimes overlook is the necessity of time. Elder Burton said:

It takes time for repentance to be final. An injury to the soul is similar to an injury to the body. Just as it takes time for a wound in the body to heal, so it also

131

takes time for a wound of the soul to heal. The deeper the cut in the body, the longer it takes to heal, and if broken bones are involved, that healing process is extended. If I cut myself, for example, the wound will gradually heal and scab over. But as it heals, it begins to itch, and if I scratch at the itching scab it will take longer to heal, for the wound will open up again. But there is a greater danger. Because of the bacteria on my fingers as I scratch the scab, the wound may become infected and I can poison the wound and can lose that part of my body and eventually even my life!

Allow injuries to follow their prescribed healing course or, if serious, see a doctor for skilled help. So it is with injuries to the soul. Allow the injury to follow its prescribed healing course without scratching it through vain regrets. If it is serious, go to your bishop and get skilled help. It may hurt as he disinfects the wound and sews the flesh together, but it will heal properly that way. Don't hurry or force it, but be patient with yourself and with your thoughts. Be active with positive and righteous thoughts and deeds. Then the wound will heal properly and you will become happy and productive again. ("Meaning of Repentance," 100)

Why does the Lord command us to repent? Not to punish us, not to humiliate us, not to impress upon us who is boss, and certainly not to make us miserable. The Savior asks of us true repentance because we are worth more to him and his Father than we can possibly comprehend:

Remember the worth of souls is great in the sight of God;

For, behold, the Lord your Redeemer suffered death in the flesh; wherefore he suffered the pain of all men, that all men might repent and come unto him.

And he hath risen again from the dead, that he might bring all men unto him, on conditions of repentance.

And how great is his joy in the soul that repenteth! (D&C 18:10–13)

I used to look at these verses in Doctrine and Covenants 18 regarding the worth of souls as "missionary" verses. I look at them a little differently now. The worth of souls is great in the sight of God because an infinite price has been paid for the redemption of all souls—for mine and for yours. We are not our own; each of us owes an infinite debt; we are bought with a tremendous price (1 Corinthians 6:19–20; 7:23). The price was paid out of love.

Jesus went to Gethsemane out of love. Jesus asks us to repent out of love—a deep and abiding love for each one of us, a love that continues even during those times when we are not so lovable.

But behold, an awful death cometh upon the wicked; for they die as to things pertaining to things of righteousness; for they are unclean, and no unclean thing can inherit the kingdom of God; but they are cast out, and consigned to partake of the fruits of their labors or of their works, which have been evil; and they drink the dregs of a bitter cup.

ALMA 40:26

# CHAPTER 7

# The Bitter Cup Ignored

As we have seen, the Savior himself gave us important insights into the nature of his supreme act of mercy in Gethsemane (D&C 19:15–19). He testified that he experienced exquisite, unbearable, and unimaginable suffering for all (D&C 18:11). The pain of all mankind was transferred to him, and he was able to act as the single substitutionary sufferer for everyone. Yet, for that vicarious suffering to work its power in our lives, each one of us must exercise faith in Jesus Christ and repent of our sins. If we do not, we will suffer exactly as the Savior did. The Savior provided an important illustration when he warned: "Wherefore, I command you again to repent, lest I humble you with my almighty power; and that you confess your sins, lest you suffer these punishments of which I have spoken, of which in the smallest, yea, even in the least degree you have tasted at the time I withdrew my Spirit" (D&C 19:20).

Martin Harris tasted such suffering and punishment when he lost the first 116 pages of manuscript that Joseph Smith had translated from the Book of Mormon plates (the book of Lehi).

Joseph also experienced the agony and torture that resulted from the withdrawal of the Lord's Spirit on that occasion. Lucy Mack Smith described as best she could, as well as mortal language is capable of describing, the feelings her son and other family members endured for only a short period:

> I well remember that day of darkness, both within and without. To us, at least, the heavens seemed clothed with blackness, and the earth shrouded with gloom. I have often said within myself, that if a continual punishment, as severe as that which we experienced on that occasion, were to be inflicted upon the most wicked characters who ever stood upon the footstool of the Almighty—if even their punishment were no greater than that, I should feel to pity their condition. (*History of Joseph Smith by His Mother*, 132)

According to the Savior himself, the anguish experienced by the Prophet Joseph Smith and Martin Harris was only a small sample (in fact, he said it was the smallest sample or least degree) of the suffering he experienced in Gethsemane. Such severe suffering is also only the smallest sample or least degree of suffering that each of us will experience if we do not repent once we come to a knowledge of God's plan for his children. This is the awful fate that awaits the wicked if they choose to ignore the Savior's atoning sacrifice.

## OTHERS LEARNED OF THE BITTER CUP

At least one other Book of Mormon prophet, King Benjamin, was familiar with the imagery of the bitter cup, which he very well may have seen in vision, considering all the other things that were revealed to him about the Messiah's ministry and mission. In the same magnificent discourse wherein he prophesied events of Jesus' life and death, King Benjamin also described the ultimate fate of the wicked, those who have rebelled against God by rejecting the call to repent and ignoring the command to exercise faith in the Lord Jesus Christ (Mosiah 3:12). He declared:

> And if they be evil they are consigned to an awful view of their own guilt and abominations, which doth cause them to shrink from the presence of the Lord into a state of misery and endless torment, from whence they can no more return; therefore they have drunk damnation to their own souls.
>
> Therefore, they have *drunk out of the cup of the wrath of God,* which justice could no more deny unto them than it could deny that Adam should fall because of his partaking of the forbidden fruit; therefore, mercy could have claim on them no more forever. (Mosiah 3:25–26; emphasis added)

King Benjamin's prophetic reference to "the cup of the wrath of God" that the wicked must consume is powerful in its vividness. The Savior himself reemphasized in our own dispensation the terrible nature of this cup when he spoke of having experienced the "fierceness of the wrath of Almighty God" (D&C 76:107; 88:106). The cup of the fierce wrath of Almighty God symbolizes God's abhorrence of sin of any kind and his retributive justice for it. When this cup was consumed by the Savior, it caused him to shrink (D&C 19:18). Likewise, those who rebel against the Savior and do not repent will drink the dregs of the bitter cup, or the cup of wrath, and shrink from the presence of God into a state of misery and endless torment. By

137

consuming the bitter cup in Gethsemane, Jesus shrank into a state of misery and torment, and being an infinite God, he experienced in that compacted time frame in Gethsemane the feelings that come to those who know their state or condition is one of "endless torment." Remember, the Savior descended below all these things (D&C 122:8).

King Benjamin was not only a mighty prophet and master teacher but also a model minister and amazing leader. When he had finished instructing his people, he followed up by checking to see if they understood his teachings and then had them commit themselves to living the doctrines and principles he had expounded (Mosiah 5:1–2). It was in this context that Benjamin's people internalized the message of the bitter cup:

> And we are willing to enter into a covenant with our God to do his will, and to be obedient to his commandments in all things that he shall command us, all the remainder of our days, that we may not bring upon ourselves a never-ending torment, as has been spoken by the angel, that we may not drink out of the cup of the wrath of God. (Mosiah 5:5)

The message of the Savior, King Benjamin, Alma, Joseph Smith, and others regarding the Savior's suffering and sacrifice in Gethsemane and on the cross is quite clear. No one who learns of the Atonement is free to ignore it. Justice demands commitment to Jesus Christ and his gospel, or else individuals must themselves suffer the fierceness of the wrath of Almighty God. C. S. Lewis observed: "You must make your choice. Either this man was, and is, the Son of God: or else a madman or something worse. You can shut Him up for a fool, you can spit at Him and kill Him as a demon; or you can fall at His feet and call Him Lord and God" (*Mere Christianity*, 56).

Once we have learned about Gethsemane, we cannot ignore it: "He has not left that open to us. He did not intend to" (Lewis, *Mere Christianity*, 56).

Elder Marion G. Romney has explained what that means in practical terms: "The gospel *requires* us to believe in the Redeemer, accept his atonement, repent of our sins, be baptized by immersion for the remission of our sins, receive the Gift of the Holy Ghost by the laying on of hands, and continue faithfully to observe, or do the best we can to observe, the principles of the gospel all the days of our lives" (Conference Report, October 1953, 36; emphasis added). That seems pretty simple and clear.

## ALL SORROW IS NOT FROM SIN

Another profound reason for embracing the Savior, his suffering and sacrifice in Gethsemane, is that all sorrow in life is not from sin. The Savior's own experience in Gethsemane helps us to see in a stunning way that not all sorrow and adversity are the result of someone having broken the commandments. Not every trial is caused by our deficient action, foolishness, or carelessness. The Savior not only knows this but appreciates it because of his experience in mortality: "Wherefore in all things it behoved him to be made like unto his brethren, that he might be made a merciful and faithful high priest" (Hebrews 2:17).

Brother Roy Doxey has written: "The Prophet Joseph Smith taught that it is a false idea to believe that the saints will escape all the judgments—disease, pestilence, war, etc.—of the last days; consequently, it is an unhallowed principle to say that these adversities are due to transgression. . . . President Joseph F.

Smith taught that it is a feeble thought to believe that the illness and affliction that come to us are attributable either to the mercy or the displeasure of God" (*Doctrine and Covenants Speaks*, 2:373).

Some trials, some tribulation and suffering, come to each of us just because of the nature of mortal life. Simply living in a fallen world produces tests, trials, pain, sickness, and affliction.

## LETTING HIM TAKE OUR BURDENS

Whatever the sources of our suffering, we know with assurance that our Father in Heaven never intended to leave us to ourselves, to let us flounder when life gets tough. As the designated substitute sufferer for us (a designation made before the foundations of this world were laid), Jesus has taken upon himself our sorrow and suffering caused by a myriad of other things besides sin. He is able to make those things work for our good, if we will let him. To the prophet Moroni, the Savior said: "And if men come unto me I will show unto them their weakness. I give unto men weakness that they may be humble; and my grace is sufficient for all men that humble themselves before me; for if they humble themselves before me, and have faith in me, then will I make weak things become strong unto them" (Ether 12:27).

Jesus Christ can make our weaknesses into strengths. He can change our minds and hearts. He can change our views and attitudes. He can change our appetites and refine our passions. He can change feelings that we sometimes can't help feeling if we are left on our own without another perspective. He can cause us to see things in new and different ways. He can heal emotional wounds as well as psychological trauma and spiritual scars. If we will pray for it and work for it, just as we pray and work when we repent, there is no heart he cannot heal. There is no problem he cannot solve. There is no sickness he cannot cure. There is no wound he cannot bind up.

Our Lord knows all things. He has all power. He has foreseen every contingency. He is not a grand cosmic laboratory experimenter who might have to run back and check the books to figure out an answer if he bumps up against a problem he has not confronted before. We can pray to him in absolute trust and confidence because he is able to answer our prayers without equivocation. We can and should go to him to find help in time of need.

Indeed, the Savior desires to help us with all our concerns and challenges, all sin, sorrow, suffering, trials, and tribulations. He himself bids us to seek his help: "Come unto me, all ye that labour and are heavy laden, and I will give you rest. Take my yoke upon you, and learn of me; for I am meek and lowly in heart: and ye shall find rest unto your souls. For my yoke is easy, and my burden is light" (Matthew 11:28–30). The word *rest*, of course, has multiple meanings. The Savior can give us rest from the weariness that life's challenges bring on, and he also lifts our vision to see that he brings rest in its greatest sense—the fulness of God's glory (D&C 84:24). He could have also said, "Come unto me, all ye that labour and are heavy laden . . . for your burdens will be light."

We come to appreciate that Jesus can deliver what he promises because he does not work in the same way other agents or influences in the world work. His ways are not our ways, and his thoughts are not our thoughts (Isaiah 55:8–9). President Ezra Taft Benson taught this general principle when he said:

The Lord works from the inside out. The world

works from the outside in. The world would take people out of the slums. Christ takes the slums out of people, and then they take themselves out of the slums. The world would mold men by changing their environment. Christ changes men who then change their environment. The world would shape human behavior, but Christ can change human nature. (*Ensign,* November 1985, 6)

Of course, a danger we face when we acknowledge the Savior's omnipotence and consuming desire to help us is the temptation to believe that prayer will give us a quick fix, that our coming to him will magically solve all our problems. Just as with overcoming sin and its effects, however, so every other challenge we face, every other sorrow, trial or pain, takes time and effort to cure or overcome. The Savior removes from us the stain of sin, but we must do the repenting. The Savior removes from us sorrow and suffering, but we must pray for it and work for it. Neither sin or tribulation go away automatically or instantaneously, at least not usually. Both involve a process.

President Benson spoke of the process of repentance and spiritual progress in a way that can serve as a model for the way in which the Lord helps us through our sorrow, suffering, and pain, and eventually removes them. He said:

We must be careful, as we seek to become more and more godlike, that we do not become discouraged and lose hope. Becoming Christlike is a lifetime pursuit and very often involves growth and change that is slow, almost imperceptible. The scriptures record remarkable accounts of men whose lives changed dramatically, in an instant, as it were: Alma the Younger,

Paul on the road to Damascus, Enos praying far into the night, King Lamoni. Such astonishing examples of the power to change even those steeped in sin give confidence that the Atonement can reach even those deepest in despair.

But we must be cautious as we discuss these remarkable examples. Though they are real and powerful, they are the exception more than the rule. For every Paul, for every Enos, and for every King Lamoni, there are hundreds and thousands of people who find the process of repentance much more subtle, much more imperceptible. Day by day they move closer to the Lord, little realizing they are building a godlike life. They live quiet lives of goodness, service, and commitment. They are like the Lamanites, who the Lord said were baptized with fire and with the Holy Ghost, *and they knew it not.* (3 Ne. 9:20; italics added.) . . .

Finally, we must remember that most repentance does not involve sensational or dramatic changes, but rather is a step-by-step, steady, and consistent movement toward godliness. (*Ensign,* October 1989, 26)

I believe the pattern President Benson describes is the pattern for the way the Lord helps us through sorrow, pain, trials, and suffering. Sometimes there is immediate deliverance, but most of the time, the results are less dramatic. We must take smaller steps of persistent, continual growth and progress. The Lord is at the helm and knows what is best for us—how to help us through our trials while accomplishing his purposes. He will get us safely home with the greatest blessing and advantage to us. We must not lose hope or confidence in our Master.

Life in the Lord is a refiner's fire. Elder James E. Faust said: "For some, the refiner's fire causes a loss of belief and faith in God, but those with eternal perspective understand that such refining is part of the perfection process" (*Ensign*, May 1979, 53).

There is another important parallel, which we cannot ignore, between repentance, or the removal of our sins, and the removal of other kinds of sorrow, suffering, pain and anguish thrust upon us from causes other than our sins. Christ removes the stain of our sins and extends forgiveness to us with the requirement that we forgive others. Likewise, other kinds of hurt, trauma, sorrow and suffering will not go away until we have extended forgiveness to others, including those who have offended us. Joseph Smith experienced the bitter cup, or the "cup of gall," as he referred to it, many times in his life—most of them not of his own making. He knew better than most the contradictions and unfairness of life. He sought to do the Lord's will but was met with horrible treatment. Yet, like the Savior, the Prophet was quick to extend mercy and forgiveness to those who sought it, even if they had caused significant injury and harm to himself and the Lord's work.

One example is the treacherous betrayal of the Prophet and the Saints in Missouri by W. W. Phelps. Nonetheless, Joseph extended his sincere forgiveness when the penitent Phelps came around. In language recalling images of the Savior in Gethsemane, the Prophet wrote to Brother Phelps to welcome him back to the fold. And in so doing, Joseph allowed us a window of insight into how close to the Savior he really was, how much he truly understood Gethsemane, and how much he had internalized what transpired there. Following is part of Joseph's letter to Brother Phelps:

Dear Brother Phelps:—I must say that it is with no ordinary feelings I endeavor to write a few lines to you in answer to [your letter]; at the same time I am rejoiced at the privilege granted me.

You may in some measure realize what my feelings, as well as Elder Rigdon's and Brother Hyrum's were, when we read your letter—truly our hearts were melted into tenderness and compassion when we ascertained your resolves. . . .

It is true, that we have suffered much in consequence of your behavior—the cup of gall, already full enough for mortals to drink, was indeed filled to overflowing when you turned against us. . . .

However, the cup has been drunk, the will of our Father has been done, and we are yet alive, for which we thank the Lord. And having been delivered from the hands of wicked men by the mercy of our God, we say it is your privilege to be delivered from the powers of the adversary, be brought into the liberty of God's dear children, and again take your stand among the Saints of the Most High, and by diligence, humility, and love unfeigned, commend yourself to our God, and your God, and to the Church of Jesus Christ.

Believing your confession to be real, and your repentance genuine, I shall be happy once again to give you the right hand of fellowship, and rejoice over the returning prodigal. . . .

"Come on, dear brother, since the war is past,
For friends at first, are friends again at last."
(*History of the Church,* 4:162–64)

We must become like Jesus. We must follow the example of Joseph Smith.

## GRATITUDE FOR GETHSEMANE

None of us in this life will escape sin, trials, tribulations, pain, or suffering. To whom, then, shall we turn for the help we so desperately need? Who possesses the kind of power to fulfill all the promises of redemption and exaltation made in the scriptures? It is Jesus Christ. In him we are secure in our hope for help.

Through his experience in Gethsemane, the Savior extends his mercy to sinners and his comfort and help to the forlorn and forsaken. He can never forget us nor forsake us. I believe it is simply not in his makeup to be able to do so or even to think of doing so. What Jesus said to ancient Israel in his role as Jehovah is more applicable than ever because it describes his relationship to us: "Can a woman forget her sucking child, that she should not have compassion on the son of her womb? yea, they may forget, yet will I not forget thee" (Isaiah 49:15).

The words of the apostle Paul are equally reassuring. He too was a man who had significant acquaintance with suffering stemming from his sins as well as his actions for righteousness' sake. He said: "Who shall separate us from the love of Christ? shall tribulation, or distress, or persecution, or famine, or nakedness, or peril, or sword?" (Romans 8:35).

Because of Gethsemane, Jesus is able to be our Great Consoler. Elder Orson F. Whitney described the purpose of trials and suffering in a way that links us with the Savior's experiences in Gethsemane and on the cross: "Is not this God's purpose in causing his children to suffer? He wants them to become more like himself. God has suffered far more than man ever did or ever will, and is therefore the great source of sympathy and consolation" (*Improvement Era*, November 1918, 7).

Why would anyone choose to ignore the bitter cup? Why would anyone choose not to embrace the Savior's atonement? Why would anyone think it more advantageous to go it alone in the world or think it advisable to try to pay for one's own mistakes and sins? President Joseph Fielding Smith flatly stated that if we are rebellious and ignore the Atonement, "we will have to pay the price ourselves" (*Doctrines of Salvation*, 1:131).

But more than that, there is an infinite difference between mere repayment and complete redemption. The Savior's experience in Gethsemane not only satisfies the demands of justice by returning us to the level of non-sinfulness required for entrance into God's kingdom but actually makes justice our friend. The Savior's atonement is able to bring us back into a right relationship with God—which we call the doctrine of justification—and set us on the path of sanctification until we actually become like God. Because of Gethsemane, all of life's unfair circumstances will be made up to us. Because of Gethsemane, Jesus is able to be a merciful God and also a just and perfect God as well. Because of Gethsemane, Jesus is able to lift us to new heights and a new way of life, able to empower us, build us, and put all things right for us.

The Savior's power is of staggering, even infinite, proportions in its ability to change us and make us into something we could not otherwise become. The Savior's experience in Gethsemane removes the effects of the Fall, the bitterness of life, and allows us to glimpse heaven. Stephen Robinson put it this way:

147

All the negative aspects of human existence brought about by the Fall, Jesus Christ absorbed into himself. He experienced vicariously in Gethsemane all the private griefs and heartaches, all the physical pains and handicaps, all the emotional burdens and depressions of the human family. He knows the loneliness of those who don't fit in, or who aren't handsome or pretty. He knows what it's like to choose up teams and be the last one chosen. He knows the anguish of parents whose children go wrong. He knows these things personally and intimately because he lived them in the Gethsemane experience. Having personally lived a perfect life, he then chose to experience our imperfect lives. In that infinite Gethsemane experience, in the meridian of time, the center of eternity, he lived a billion billion lifetimes of sin, pain, disease, and sorrow.

God has no magic wand with which to simply wave bad things into nonexistence. The sins that he remits, he remits by making them his own and suffering them. The pain and heartache that he relieves, he relieves by suffering them himself. These things can be transferred, but they cannot be simply wished or waved away. They must be suffered. Thus, we owe him not only for our spiritual cleansing from sin but for our physical, mental and emotional healings as well, for he has borne these infirmities for us also. All that the Fall put wrong, the Savior in his atonement puts right. It is all part of his infinite sacrifice—of his infinite gift. (Religious Education prayer meeting, 12 February 1992)

When I wonder how and why Jesus did what he did in

Gethsemane, when I try to take it all in, to absorb the infinite, I am reduced to inadequate expressions. To use Elder Neal A. Maxwell's phrase, Gethsemane was "enormity multiplied by infinity" (*Ensign*, May 1985, 78). I cannot succinctly explain the how and why. And then I realize that no more profound words were probably ever spoken than by my little friend Brittany: "That's Jesus, and he loves us. All of us!"

# Sources

Aldous, Edwin W. "A Reflection on the Atonement's Healing Power." *Ensign*, April 1987.

Andrus, Hyrum L. *God, Man, and the Universe.* Salt Lake City: Bookcraft, 1968.

Burton, Theodore M. "The Meaning of Repentance." In *Devotional and Fireside Speeches.* Provo, Utah: Brigham Young University Press, 1985.

Cannon, George Q. *Gospel Truth: Two Volumes in One.* Edited by Jerreld L. Newquist. Salt Lake City: Deseret Book, 1987.

Clark, J. Reuben, Jr. *Behold the Lamb of God: Selections from the Sermons and Writings, Published and Unpublished, of J. Reuben Clark, Jr., on the Life of the Savior.* Salt Lake City: Deseret Book, 1962.

*Collected Discourses.* Edited by Brian H. Stuy. 5 vols. Sandy, Utah: B.H.S. Publishing, 1992.

Dibble, Jonathan A. "Delivered by the Power of God." *Ensign*, October 1987.

Doxey, Roy W. *The Doctrine and Covenants Speaks.* 2 vols. Salt Lake City: Deseret Book, 1970.

Edwards, William D., Wesley J. Gabel, and Floyd E. Hosmer. "On the Physical Death of Jesus Christ." *Journal of the American Medical Association* 225, no. 11 (March 21, 1986): 1455.

Eusebius. *The Ecclesiastical History*. Vol. 1. Translated by Kirsopp Lake. Cambridge, Mass.: Harvard University Press, 1992.

Ginzberg, Louis. *Legends of the Jews*. Philadelphia: Jewish Publication Society of America, 1937–66.

Hareuveni, Nogah. *Nature in Our Biblical Heritage*. Kiryat Ono, Israel: Neot Kedumim Ltd., 1981.

Hinckley, Bryant S. *Sermons and Missionary Services of Melvin Joseph Ballard*. Salt Lake City: Deseret Book, 1949.

*Hymns of The Church of Jesus Christ of Latter-day Saints*. Salt Lake City: The Church of Jesus Christ of Latter-day Saints, 1985.

Kimball, Spencer W. *Tragedy or Destiny?* Salt Lake City: Deseret Book, 1977.

Jackson, Kent P., ed. *1 Nephi to Alma 29*. Vol. 7 of *Studies in Scripture* series. Salt Lake City: Deseret Book, 1987.

*Journal of Discourses*. 26 vols. London: Latter-day Saints' Book Depot, 1854–86.

Lewis, C. S. *Mere Christianity*. New York: Touchstone, 1980.

Maxwell, Neal A. *Deposition of a Disciple*. Salt Lake City: Deseret Book, 1976.

———. *Lord, Increase Our Faith*. Salt Lake City: Bookcraft, 1994.

McConkie, Bruce R. *Doctrinal New Testament Commentary*. 4 vols. Salt Lake City: Bookcraft, 1965.

———. *Mormon Doctrine*. 2d ed. Salt Lake City: Bookcraft, 1966.

———. *The Promised Messiah*. Salt Lake City: Deseret Book, 1978.

Murphy-O'Connor, Jerome. "What Really Happened in Gethsemane." *Bible Review* 14 (April 1998): 28–39, 52.

Robinson, Stephen E. Address to Religious Education prayer meeting, Brigham Young University, Provo, Utah, 12 February 1992.

Rosen, Ceil, and Moishe Rosen. *Christ in the Passover: Why Is This Night Different?* Chicago, Ill.: Moody Press, 1978.

Smith, Joseph. *History of The Church of Jesus Christ of Latter-day Saints*. Edited by B. H. Roberts. 2d ed. rev. 7 vols. Salt Lake City: The Church of Jesus Christ of Latter-day Saints, 1932–51.

———. *Lectures on Faith*. Salt Lake City: Deseret Book, 1985.

———. *Teachings of the Prophet Joseph Smith*. Selected by Joseph Fielding Smith. Salt Lake City: Deseret Book, 1970.

Smith, Joseph F. *Gospel Doctrine*. Salt Lake City: Deseret Book, 1966.

Smith, Joseph Fielding. *Doctrines of Salvation*. 3 vols. Salt Lake City: Bookcraft, 1954–56.

Smith, Lucy Mack. *History of Joseph Smith by His Mother*. Edited by Preston Nibley. Salt Lake City: Bookcraft, 1945.

Talmage, James E. *Jesus the Christ*. Salt Lake City: Deseret Book, 1913.

Whitney, Orson F. *Improvement Era*, November 1918.

———. *Through Memory's Halls*. Independence, Mo.: Zion's Printing and Publishing, 1930.

# Index